THE
TESTIMONY
OF
ST. JOHN

INCLUDES A
SIDE-BY-SIDE COMPARISON
WITH THE
KING JAMES VERSION

First Edition
Text v1.307 - 2021.04.30

Hard Cover ISBN 9781951168797
Soft Cover ISBN 9781951168780

Published in the United States by
Restoration Archive LLC

Restoration Scriptures Foundation is a trademark of
Restoration Archive LLC

The Restoration Archive website address:
www.restorationarchives.com

TABLE OF CONTENTS

Preface

This edition of the Testimony of St. John is presented as part of the ongoing restoration of the Gospel of Jesus Christ. New light and truth is coming forward in our day, including revelation foretold in prophecy.

The Testimony of St. John found in this volume, along with many additional treasures of the ongoing restoration can be found inside the third volume of the Restoration Edition Scriptures called "Teachings and Commandments." The Testimony of St. John is provided here in a stand-alone version for easy study and sharing. The reader is invited to search and study this testimony, and encouraged to investigate and enjoy the light and truth found in the full Restoration Edition of the scriptures. See here for more information:

> Digital Editions: scriptures.info
> Print Editions: scriptures.shop

Also included in this volume is an Appendix containing a side-by-side comparative study of the Testimony of St. John and King James Version (KJV) of The Gospel according to St. John from the New Testament for the reader to harmonize the different versions of John's testimony found in scripture. It is hoped that this comparison format will reveal many insightful and enlightening differences to the attentive reader. Ultimately the intent of this work is to offer light and truth and point towards our Lord Jesus Christ and the restoration of His gospel that continues in our day.

Introduction

In 2016 the Restoration Edition of the Scriptures was being compiled as part of a major effort to recover and preserve the "fullness of the scriptures" that the Lord had commanded Joseph Smith to prepare (see Teachings and Commandments 26:5 and Glossary: Fullness of the Scriptures).[1] Joseph was murdered before he could complete the work and publish it. Following his death, some parts of his work were variously published as the "Joseph Smith Translation" (JST) or "Inspired Version" (IV) of the Bible. However, all of these efforts fell short of including all of the corrections and clarifications Joseph had made while he was alive, and they all added additional, uninspired material that did not originate with Joseph at all.

The Restoration Edition includes every known emendation, correction, explanation and revision of the Bible made by Joseph Smith during his lifetime. However, because Joseph was not able to complete the project and publish it, despite our best efforts the Scriptures are still incomplete and contain errors.

While reviewing the progress of the ongoing recovery effort at that time, I had the impression that a new translation of John's Gospel was needed. I asked a qualified Greek scholar to undertake that project and he declined. But the impression remained that it nevertheless needed to be done.

I made it the subject of prayer and was told to do the work. I spent a few days working with an English-Greek New Testament, the JS Translation of John, and a Greek Lexicon before becoming hopelessly discouraged by the many word-meaning options and language phrasing choices. I prayed about it before retiring for the night and essentially quit. I explained that it would take years for me to accomplish this, and that I was not going to be able to solve the riddles of the text without long study, far longer than the time expected to see the Restoration Edition of the Scriptures completed. I went to bed assuming I was done with it.

---

[1] Unless otherwise noted, all scriptural references in this work cite to the Restoration Edition (RE) of the Scriptures, published by the Restoration Scriptures Foundation.

In the middle of that night I was awakened and given the solution to every dilemma I had been facing in the work on the text. So the next day I continued on from where I had abandoned the work and, to my surprise, everything was opened to my mind so clearly and continuously that the entire project was completed in less than three weeks. The light of heaven opened the material in a way I had never thought of nor had previously attained to in considering the Gospel of John. At times it progressed so rapidly that I was unable to finish one part before the next came rolling out. Many new and different things were added, and at least one thing was dropped entirely because it was not part of John's original composition.

Because of the rapid way it rolled out, once I finished the text I went back to clean up a lot of what had been left as incomplete or run-on sentences, missing words (particularly conjunctions) and cryptic or inadequate explanations. The intent of the writer, John, was revealed, including why some things were included in the text and the manner he wrote. When it began it was an attempt at a "translation" but by the time it was completed it was clearly a "revelation" and not merely a translation of a text. Therefore the result does not have my name on it, because I cannot claim any credit for the content. I failed in what I was attempting. What resulted came from heaven.

The place where it became hopelessly discouraging was the marriage at Cana. At that point the text was capable of so many different word choices that it would require a great deal of study and prayer to get it correct. I knew it would be impossible for me to accomplish this project in any meaningful time frame. The revealed solution to that part of the text surprised and enlightened me. The mind of John was nimble, brilliant and subtle–capable of composing at multiple levels at the same time.

There was one part of the record I fought to keep out, so that I could answer inquiries about whether this was the completed record of John–I could then say, "No, it's not complete." I fought to eliminate one part of that story that I did not personally want to see in there, but the project couldn't be done until it was added. It was the last thing reluctantly added, and it is in there.

I don't assert or claim interpretive authority over the text. I will testify to you that the text is a revelation, that it came from God, that it is a gift given to us, and it is His (God's). Ultimately, everything that is part of the Gospel narrative belongs to the Lord, and therefore, I believe it would be a mistake for me to begin to announce interpretations related to a document when I don't believe that I own that right. If I do so, I run the risk of cutting off other people's insight or inspired reading of a text that may bless and benefit me if I were to hear it. If I close their mind, if I shut their mouths, if I get out ahead of them when they have the right to do so, then I'm the poorer for that, and you are the poorer too. Joseph Smith once said that he may have made a lot of mistakes, but there's no mistakes in the revelations. That was his way of saying they are not his property.

One question I've been asked is whether the event involving the woman taken in adultery happened, since it is not in the Testimony of John. My understanding is that the incident involving the Lord and the woman taken in adultery really did happen. It was a well-known story that had been handed down all the way back from New Testament times, but it was never in the record of John. As it turns out, the only place that we have it is in the version of the Gospel of John that's been handed down to us. But that got added by a monk who, like everyone else, believed the story to be authentic. Everyone believed the story to be trustworthy, but it wasn't in any of the gospel accounts. Therefore, a copyist put it into John's gospel, but John didn't originally put it in there. Accordingly, I did not put it into the Testimony of St. John. But I don't doubt the incident happened, and I don't doubt that the Lord handled it in the way in which it's told. It's just not John's story.

There are a few clarifications in the new volume of scriptures that were prepared that are not found elsewhere in previously existing canons of scripture. One of those is the clarification that a new dispensation mandates a new baptism. And it's found in the Testimony of St. John in the exchange between Nicodemus and Christ, where he's making inquiry and Christ essentially says, "Your ordinance work will not suffice." (Because they were practicing baptism, no one went to John the Baptist and said, "Why are you baptizing?" They went to John the Baptist and asked, "What authority are you using to do your baptism?" because baptism was a common thing.)

When Nicodemus went to Christ in the Testimony of St. John, Christ clarifies that a new dispensation mandates new baptism. That shows up in the Teachings and Commandments as a revelation, where it says your dead works under your old law won't be accepted; new baptism is required, even if you've been previously baptized a hundred times. Once a new dispensation begins, it mandates that there be a new baptism that takes place. There are other important details that are found in the new Scriptures that are completely missing from the previously existing canon of Scripture, now preserved in the Restoration Edition.

This Testimony of St. John adds truth and light that confirms old truths, reveals new ones, and shows the Lord's continuing mercy for us.

Denver Snuffer, Jr.
September 20, 2021

Prologue

John was shown Christ's entire development as the Son of God and testified of how He gained the status. His testimony included this description of Christ:

> And I, John, bear record that I beheld his glory, as the glory of the Only Begotten of the Father, full of grace and truth, even the Spirit of Truth which came and dwelt in the flesh, and dwelt among us.
>
> And I, John, saw that he received not of the fullness at the first, but received grace for grace. And he received not of the fullness at first, but continued from grace to grace until he received a fullness, and thus he was called, the Son of God, because he received not of the fullness at the first. (T&C 93:3-4, see also D&C 93:12-14)

Although most people read this to be only a description of Christ's earthly progression, John states he is testifying to what he saw of Christ's progression before His life on this earth. He states:

> I saw his glory, that he was in the beginning, before the world was. (Ibid. v. 2)

The testimony of John should be read as a description of Christ's progression in both the pre-existence and here on earth. (See Snuffer, Denver, Jr., *Eighteen Verses* p. 157)

THE
TESTIMONY
OF
ST. JOHN

Below is a newly revealed account of John the Beloved's Testimony of Jesus the Messiah, given through Denver Snuffer Jr. during the month of January 2017.

Chapter 1

I n the Highest Council of Heaven there was One who spoke out. And the One who spoke out was among the Gods, and He was a God. He was in the Council of the Gods, and the creation of the cosmos was organized through Him. And without Him does not exist one thing that has come into existence in the cosmos. In Him was the power of life and this power was conveyed into the cosmos as the Light in men and every thing. The Light shone in the chaos and those in darkness have not been able to grasp it.

2 There was a man sent from God and his name was John. This man was sent as a witness so that he might testify and identify the Light to give everyone a reason to believe through the Messiah. He, John, was not the Light, but he was sent by Heaven as a witness to testify of the Light, and to end the dispensation of Moses, and baptize to begin a new dispensation. The Light enlightens every man who is progressing upward in the cosmos.

3 The Messenger of the Heavenly Council was in the cosmos, and the cosmos existed through Him, and the cosmos had not acquired His knowledge. He came into His own creation, but those there were unable to understand Him. As many as perceived the Light in Him, to them He gave knowledge to enable them to follow the path to become like Him, begotten children in the family of the Most High God. This is only possible for those who believe through His name. Those who believe through His name are no longer born of blood to follow the appetites of flesh, nor the ambitions of man, but are able to become, like Him, the offspring of God. This one who was Spokesman from the Heavenly Council was made flesh, and He temporarily cast His tent among us, and we

could see His knowledge of the path to ascend in light and truth, he was a member of the Family of God, full of the power to ascend and able to display truth to others.

4 John bore witness of him, and proclaimed, This is He of whom I testified; He who would be born after me has advanced in progression above me. He has advanced in progression far beyond everyone else in this sphere. For in the Council of Heaven was the Spokesman, even God's Heir, who is born into the flesh and sent to us to fulfill the will of the Father. And as many as obtain authority in His name shall gain the right to ascend to Heaven. We who have witnessed His fullness comprehend what Eternal life means through Him revealing the pathway of ascension to the Throne of God. For the law was given through Moses, but life and truth come through Jesus the Messiah. The law gave carnal instructions, but led only to condemnation and death. The gospel is to empower endless life, through Jesus the Messiah, the Only Begotten Son, who is a manifestation of the love of the Father. No man has seen the Father without hearing Him testify of the Son, for only through Him is any soul saved.

5 And this was the witness of John, when the Jews sent priests and Levites from Jerusalem to inquire, Who are you? And he did not deny that he possessed the Spirit of God's messenger, but declared, I am not the Messiah. And they asked him, How then do you possess the Spirit of God's messenger? And he said, I am not that messenger foretold to come and restore all things.

6 And they asked him, Are you the prophet Moses said God would raise up from among Israel, like unto Moses, in whose mouth God would put His words and he shall speak all that God commands him? And it will come to pass that whosoever does not hearken to that prophet, God will judge. Do you claim to be that prophet? And he answered, No.

7 Then they asked, Who then are you? We are obligated to convey your answer to them that sent us. What do you say for yourself? He said, I am a voice of one crying in the wilderness, Make straight the way of the Lord, as predicted would be sent by the prophet Isaiah.

8 And the inquirers who were Pharisees asked him, Why then are you baptizing if you are not the Messiah, nor come as the messen-

ger to restore all things, nor the prophet foretold by Moses to whom we must give heed? John answered, I baptize with water, but there is one standing among you, whom you do not acknowledge and I bear testimony of him. He is the one foretold by Moses, and he will preach following my witness of him. He has progressed beyond me so much that in comparison I am not worthy to kneel before him; his shoe's latchet I am not worthy to unloose, nor am I worthy to wash his feet. I could never substitute for him. He will baptize, not only with water, but also with fire and with the Holy Ghost.

9 The next day John beheld Jesus coming to him, and said to those who were with him, Behold the Sacrificial Lamb of God, who will redeem from the fall of the creation! And John testified of him to the others, saying, This is him I described before, saying, After me will come a man who has progressed far beyond me, for he existed before me in Heaven. I recognize him, and testify to Israel that he is that Prophet foretold by Moses to whom all must give heed. Therefore I am here baptizing with water to prepare people for him.

10 And John recounted, When I baptized him, I saw the Spirit descending from Heaven in a sign of a dove, and it abode upon him. I recognized him as God's Son because God, who sent me, and commanded me to baptize to prepare people to hear him, told me, On the man you see the Spirit descend in a sign of a dove and remain with him, he will be the one sent to bestow the Holy Ghost. I saw this happen, and testify that he is the Son of God.

11 The foregoing events happened in Bethabara beyond Jordan, as John baptized there.

12 On the next day after, John stood beside two of his followers, and noticing Jesus as he walked nearby, he said to the two others, Behold the Sacrificial Lamb of God! And these two who had followed John, when they heard that testimony, followed after Jesus. Then Jesus turned, and saw them following him, and asked, What do you want? They called him, Rabbi (which means acknowledged teacher), and asked, How can we understand the truth and advance? He replied, All men move upward by gaining light. If you advance you will learn to be like me. And these two went with him and were taught, and were his companions through that day, for it

was mid-afternoon. One of the two who heard the testimony of John and followed Jesus was Andrew, Simon Peter's brother. That evening he went to his brother Simon and said to him, We have found the Messiah! And he brought Peter to Jesus. And when Jesus beheld him, he said, You are Simon, the son of Jonah. You will be called Cephas, which is, by interpretation, a seer, or a stone. And these men were fishermen, but they immediately left every thing else behind to follow Jesus.

13 The day following Jesus went to Galilee, and encountered Philip, and said to him, Follow me. Now Philip was at Bethsaida, the residence also of Andrew and Peter. Philip found Nathanael and said to him, We have found the Prophet that Moses foretold in the law, and who the prophets promised would come, Jesus of Nazareth, the son of Joseph.

14 And Nathanael asked him, Can the promised Messiah come from Nazareth? Philip said to him, Come and see. Jesus saw Nathanael coming to meet him, and said of him, Behold a pure Israelite indeed, in whom is no guile! Nathanael asked him, How do you know anything about me? Jesus answered him, Before Philip called you, when you were praying under the fig tree, I heard your prayer. Nathanael responded, Rabbi, you must be the Son of God. You are the King of Israel. Jesus responded to him, You believe in me because I said to you that I heard your prayer under the fig tree? You will see greater things than these. And he said to him, In the name of Father Ahman I promise you, Hereafter you shall see the fiery ascent to Heaven open, and the angels of God ascending and descending to visit the Son of Man.

15 On the third day of the week, there was a marriage in Cana of Galilee; and the mother of Jesus was there. Jesus and his followers were invited guests at the marriage. And when the wedding party wanted more wine, his mother said to him, They have run out of wine. Jesus replied, Mother, why are you talking to me about it? The time for me to provide sacramental wine has not yet arrived. But his mother instructed the servants, Whatever he tells you to do, follow through with it.

16 There were six waterpots made of stone that were used for ceremonial purification in religious observances, each containing twenty to thirty gallons. Jesus instructed the servants, Fill the wa-

terpots with water. And they filled them up to the brim. And he said, Now remove some and take it to the host. And they took it to him. When the host of the wedding tasted the ceremonial water, it had been converted to wine. But he did not know the source that converted the water, unlike the servants who recognized the Source. The host of the feast called for the bridegroom, and praised him using a proverb, saying, Careful men introduce their plans using the best wine, and later, when their followers are drunk, then their worst – but you have brought us better wine than at the start.

17 This was a sign confirming his role as the Messiah that was performed by Jesus in Cana of Galilee. It was a demonstration of authority over both the elements and ordinances of salvation. Those who recognized this as a sign of his authority were awed as they considered it was him present among them.

18 After this he went down to Capernaum, he, his mother, his brothers, and his disciples, and they were there a few days. As the Passover arrived, Jesus traveled up to Jerusalem where in the temple, there were appointed traders selling oxen, sheep, and doves, and others exchanged coins to profit from the temple donations. Seeing this, Jesus made a whip using small cords, and he drove the profiteers out of the temple, and also their sheep and oxen; and dumped out the exchangers' money, and turned over the tables; and confronted those who were profiteering from Passover, saying, Get your business out of here and do not degrade my Father's house to merely your place of business. It reminded his disciples of the Psalm, The zeal of thy house hath eaten me up.

19 The temple authorities, who had authorized the profiteering, confronted Jesus asking, If you think you have a right to exercise authority over the temple, while identifying yourself as God's son, show us a sign to prove you have this right, so we can believe you. Jesus answered and said, I will replace the holy of holies in three days with a new holy House of God. The Jews declared, It took forty-six years to build this temple, and will you replace it in three days? But he was talking of the temple of his resurrected body. Later after he was resurrected from the dead, his disciples remembered he had said this to the temple authorities, and they remembered the scripture, and what Jesus had said to the disciples.

²⁰ Now while he was in Jerusalem at the Passover many believed on his name when they saw the healing miracles he did. But Jesus did not attempt to have them pledge loyalty to him because he knew they were fickle, and miracles alone cannot produce faith, because sign-seekers are wicked and adulterous.

Chapter 2

There was a Pharisee named Nicodemus, a member of the Sanhedrin, who was in darkness and came to visit with Jesus. He sought wisdom from Jesus and said, Enlightened heavenly guide, some of us know you have descended from the High Council of Heaven because signs confirm you have authority from God. Jesus answered and said to him, In the name of Father Ahman I testify there is a new dispensation begun. You must accept the ordinances of this new Light or you cannot hope to progress to know God.

2 Nicodemus said to him, If I believe this, can I ascend in this life, or will it be accomplished only in the afterlife? Jesus answered, In the name of Father Ahman I say to you, Except you receive the ordinance of baptism to join the new dispensation, and thereby forsake your sins and receive forgiveness and an outpouring of the Spirit, you will not ascend to God's presence in this life or the life to come. All who are devoted to the ambitions of the flesh remain imprisoned by the flesh, and those who are born anew through the ordinances, receive the Spirit of Truth, and are able to know the record of Heaven by the Spirit of Truth. Do not question if what I say is true because the Spirit of Truth confers light, knowledge, and understanding of the mysteries of Heaven within every soul who receives it.

3 Nicodemus replied to him, Why is this not widely known? Jesus answered, Why does a member of the Sanhedrin not recognize that a new dispensation has begun? In the name of Father Ahman I confirm what was told by John the Baptist and I have begun a work that comes from Heaven. But you who lead Israel fight against it and you refuse to humble yourselves. If I offered you a position of respect and authority, as you now hold, you would believe. But because I testify only of heavenly things that require faith and sacrifice, you refuse to believe? I tell you, if you want to ascend to the Heavenly Council, you must first acknowledge and give heed to the messengers sent by them. You can refuse to believe, but you will see in me a sign and remember this saying: When Moses nailed a brass serpent upon a pole in the wilderness, he prophesied of me. And I shall also be nailed upon a tree, and those who believe on me will receive deliverance through my sacrifice, even as Israel was delivered by looking with faith at Moses' serpent.

4 Father Ahman loves the world, and like father Abraham, Father Ahman will allow His Son to become an offering for sin. Whoever believes and follows His Son will not be lost, but have everlasting life. For God did not send His Son into the world to condemn the world, but to save the world. Those who believe and follow His Son will escape the limitations of sin. The faithless are condemned already because they refuse to believe and obey the Only Begotten Son of God. Every thing about my assignment, which I am now performing, was foretold by the prophets sent earlier to teach Israel, for they all testified of me. They told you I would come, and I am now here doing what was prophesied, but you refuse to see it happening. Enough is underway that rejecting it means you prefer darkness to light. Humble yourself and admit the prophets foretold the very things now underway; repent and be baptized and the Spirit of Truth will open your eyes. If you want greater light, you will obey this instruction. If you refuse, then you never meant it when you greeted me as an enlightened heavenly guide.

Chapter 3

After this Jesus and his disciples went to the land of Judea, and while there he taught, dined and worshipped with, and baptized them. John the Baptist was also baptizing north of there in Aenon, near to Salim, where the water was plentiful at that time of year. Crowds continued to go to John, and this occurred before he was imprisoned.

2 A controversy arose between traditionalist Jews and John's followers about authority to baptize. The traditionalists hoped to have John denounce Jesus baptizing. They went to John, hoping to turn his answer against Jesus. They asked John, The man you baptized beyond Jordan now is also baptizing and drawing away people to follow him, but he has not been given authority by us or by you.

3 John answered and said, Authority comes from Heaven, to both him and to me. I told you I am not the Messiah, but I have been sent to prepare the way for the Messiah. I am only like a guest at another man's wedding, and not the groom. But I rejoice to be in the groom's company. Jesus is the groom. He is the one whose mission is the more important. He must increase, but I must decrease. I have come to end an era in Israel, but he has come to begin another. He descended from Heaven to serve here, and all of us need to acknowledge him – I not only refuse to deny his authority, I confirm it.

4 Because John the Baptist saw and heard Jesus identified by Heaven as the Messiah, he testified boldly of him. But few people were willing to accept John's testimony about Jesus. Despite that, his testimony was true. God made John a witness and therefore John's witness was binding. Jesus was a messenger sent from the Heavenly Council to declare the truth, and Jesus had limitless access to the record of Heaven, the truth of all things, the light that quickens every thing. He is the one Moses prophesied would come and all Israel must give him heed or be cut off. God the Father loves and acknowledges Jesus as His Son, and has made him the steward over all creation. We are required to acknowledge God's Son to be rescued by him, for only the Son can rescue us from the Fall of Adam. Jesus lived as the example, proving the pattern for redemption from the Fall as he progressed from grace to grace, until he re-

ceived a fullness, or in other words, grew in light and truth until he was filled with truth and stands as the light of the world.

5 When the Pharisees learned that Jesus made and baptized more disciples than John, and that John's popularity could not be turned against Jesus, they conspired about how to have both John and Jesus executed. Some of the Pharisees thought John might be a prophet, but none of them believed on Jesus, whom they rejected and did not respect. Jesus recognized this was how they viewed him.

6 Unlike John the Baptist, Jesus baptized only a few people, instead preferring that his followers perform the rite and learn to minister. When he left Judea to return to Galilee, he informed his followers that he was required to visit Samaria on the way.

Chapter 4

He next went to the city of Shechem in Samaria, at the foot of Mt. Gerizim, adjacent to the parcel of ground which Joseph inherited from his father Jacob, which is the place where Jacob's well was located. Jesus was tired from the journey, it being about midday, and he sat down on the wall of the well. A woman of Samaria came to draw water. Jesus asked her, Could you give to me a drink?

2 His followers were not with him, but had left to buy food in the city and therefore he was alone. The Samaritan woman replied to him, I do not understand why a Jew would ask me as a Samaritan to give you a drink. Jews look down on us as unclean, so why would you ask me such a thing?

3 Jesus replied, I have been sent by God, and if you recognized who now asks you to give a drink of water, you would gladly do so and ask me in turn for the gift of living water. The woman responded to him, Sir, you have nothing to reach the water, and the well is deep, so how can you suggest you could offer living water? Are you greater than our father Jacob, to whom God gave this well, who drank here with his children, and he watered his cattle from this source? Jesus answered her, Whoever drinks water from this well will thirst again, but whoever drinks from the living water which I shall give him shall live from eternity to eternity, for the Source in me will be the power to rise upward forever, worlds without end.

4 The woman said unto him, Sir, give me of the water that I no longer will thirst nor need to come here to draw from this well. Jesus said unto her, Go, get your husband and I will teach you together. The woman replied, I have no husband (she spoke of herself). Jesus said to her, You are right, even though you have had five husbands (he meant this of both her and also the Samaritans whose Israelite blood was mixed with five other nations), and the man you live with presently has not married you (meaning both her and her province). So you are correct saying you have no husband. The woman said unto him, Sir, you speak like you are a prophet. Our fathers, the patriarchs, were visited by God on this mountain, where later the first tabernacle was set up. But the Jews claim that God's only temple is in Jerusalem. Jesus said to her, Woman, remember this saying: The time will come when neither

on this mountain nor at Jerusalem will be the place to worship. Worship the Father through me.

5 You Samaritans do not understand God, although you claim to worship Him. Those who follow me know how to worship. Salvation does not belong to the Jews, but instead will come from a Messiah rejected by the Jews. The hour has arrived when the true worshipers are being taught how to worship the Father in spirit and in truth, for the Father wants mankind to know Him. The Father will share his Spirit with those who know him. His Spirit is truth and light. And they who worship him must worship in spirit and in truth.

6 The woman said to him, I know that a Messiah is prophesied to come, and when he comes he will restore all that has been lost since the time of Adam. Jesus responded, I am he: I am come to restore, to repair, to redeem, and I am come to gather.

7 As he was talking with the woman his followers arrived and were surprised to see that he talked with this Samaritan woman, but no one questioned him about why he would teach and testify openly to her. The woman then abandoned her waterpot, and quickly went into the city to proclaim to them about who was at the well. She testified to the men, Come see a man who spoke as a seer. I testify that he is the Messiah and ask you to come hear him for yourselves. Because she was influential, a great crowd went out to investigate the woman's testimony of him.

8 In the meantime, his disciples brought food and told him that he ought to eat. But seeing the approaching crowd he said, I have food to eat you do not see. His companions asked one another, Has someone brought him food while we were gone? Jesus clarified, My strength comes by obeying the will of God who sent me to do his work. Doing that sustains me by his Holy Spirit, and protects me until I finish his work. Do not make the mistake of thinking there are four months still before the harvest. I want you to look at the approaching crowd. They are the field I have been sent to harvest; they are prepared and ready. For this reason I have come to this place. These people will accept a new dispensation and the truth. Anyone who helps me with the Father's work in harvesting souls will likewise save their own soul. The harvest saves both the planter and gatherer together. Remember the expression: One

plants and another harvests. I send you to help with the harvest, but others have prepared this field. The prophets planted and these people have responded, and you join the labor of the prophets by now teaching these prepared people.

9 Many of the Samaritans from Shechem accepted him because of the woman's testimony that he was a seer who prophesied to and about her. So when the Samaritan crowd came to hear him, they implored him to stay and teach them. And he stayed and taught for two days. Then many more believed because of what he taught. Then others said to the woman, Now we no longer depend on your testimony, but we have heard him teach us, and recognize that this is indeed the Messiah, the Savior who has come to rescue the world.

10 Jesus stayed two days with them teaching, worshipping, and having them baptized before he departed to return to Galilee. On the way home Jesus repeated the parable: A prophet is never honored in his home town. But when he arrived in Galilee, the Galileans were excited to see him because many of them had been at Jerusalem during the Passover and told the others about the miracles he did there.

11 Jesus came again into Cana of Galilee, where he earlier had turned water into wine. There was a wealthy and respected man there whose son lay sick at Capernaum. When he heard that Jesus had come back from Judea to Galilee, he traveled to Galilee to beg him to come to his home at Capernaum and heal his son because the young man was near death. Jesus responded to him, Like other Jews who seek signs, you want me to physically travel to him and put on a display, but all that is necessary is for you to have faith in the power to heal. But the father begged, Sir, please come to my house so that my child does not die. Jesus replied, Go to your home without me, for your son will recover and live – I have faith this will happen even if you do not. And the man wanted to believe what Jesus said, and trusting it may be possible, he left to return home. While he traveled back to his house, his servants were hurrying to meet him, and said, Your son has recovered and is not going to die! The father asked them when his recovery began. The servants told him it was the day before, just after midday. The father knew this had been the very moment when Jesus spoke the words that his son would recover and live, and he realized Jesus

was a messenger of God. And his entire family likewise shared this belief in Jesus. This was the second miracle Jesus performed when he returned from Judea to Galilee.

[12] After this came the Feast of the Tabernacles, and Jesus made the pilgrimage to Jerusalem for the feast.

Chapter 5

Now there is at Jerusalem, by the sheep market, a pool, named in Hebrew, Bethesda, where there were five porches. In these porches lay a great many disabled people who were blind, infirm, or lame, hoping for people to take pity on them. There was one man among them who had been lame for thirty-eight years. Jesus noticed him in particular, and knew that he had been afflicted for many years. He asked him, Do you want to be made whole? The man answered him, Sir, I would be grateful for any help. Jesus replied to him, Arise, take up your bedding and go forward. And as soon as Jesus spoke, the man was made whole, and picked up his bedding, and walked. But this happened on the Jewish Sabbath day. The Jews were therefore judgmental and confronted the man who was cured, accusing him, saying, It is the Sabbath day, it is not lawful for you to carry your bedding. He answered them, The man who restored me, said to me, Pick up your bedding and walk. Then the angry Jews said, Who told you, Pick up your bedding and walk? But the healed man was unable to identify who healed him because Jesus had walked away and mingled with the festival crowd. Shortly afterwards Jesus met him again in the temple, and said to him, Remember, you have been healed, but take care to follow God, do not be ungrateful or you will offend God. Those who were following and watching Jesus (for the Jews were on the watch for him when he entered Jerusalem) were told by the man that Jesus was his healer.

2 Then these Jews were even more angry at Jesus, and conspired to kill him because he had violated their traditions about the Sabbath and they feared he did every thing to undermine their authority. But Jesus corrected them saying, My Father works on every day including the Sabbath, and I follow his example. This convinced the Jews to be even more determined to kill Jesus, because he had both violated their traditions about the Sabbath, and claimed God was his Father, which would make him equal with God.

3 Then Jesus affirmed to them, In the name of Father Ahman I tell you, The Son does nothing of himself, but I am following the path that my Father walks. Every thing the Father has done, I am likewise to do. My Father loves His Son, and has revealed to me every thing he has done, and I have a work to do for me to finish the path of my Father. You may not believe me, but before the end you will

be in awe of what I am sent to do. The Father has attained to the resurrection, and I am sent to do likewise. In this creation the Father has made me the Source and judge of the resurrection. You will be required to honor the Son, even as you honor the Father. Anyone who disrespects the Son also disrespects the Father who sent me.

4 In the name of Father Ahman I testify to you, He who hearkens to my testimony, and trusts him who sent me, there is no end to his potential progression. His progress will not cease, for I demonstrate the pathway of Eternal lives.

5 In the name of Father Ahman I testify to you, The time has arrived when even the spirits in Sheol will hear the voice of the Son of God. Those who hearken to my testimony shall also progress upward on the pathway. The Father has the power of endless life within himself, and he has empowered the Son to attain this identical state through progression on his pathway. I hold authority to judge mankind because I am Son Ahman. Do not doubt this, for the time is fast approaching when the dead will also be taught by my voice. The dead will rise from the grave: first the faithful in the resurrection of the just, and then the faithless in the resurrection of the unjust. Every soul will be judged by Son Ahman. Whatever the Father tells me, I accept and teach, and my teachings are all just and true. I take nothing on myself apart from the Father's instruction. I do not pursue my own agenda, but the Father's agenda, for I act under his authority.

6 Therefore I am a witness of the truth, and my witness is true. I am not a lone witness because my Father testifies to those who will listen. My works testify also. But you do not listen to my Father and you condemn my works. Therefore you reject the truth. You asked John, and he was also my witness of the truth. He did not receive his testimony from only a man, but directly from God, and you admit he is a prophet. Therefore you should accept his testimony.

7 I am telling you these things to save you. John was a brilliant light sent from above, and you were willing to hear and acknowledge him for a short while. But there is even a greater reason than John's words to believe what I teach: As I complete the journey to finish the Father's path, those final steps will plainly testify of me.

8 I testify of the truth. The Father testifies to those who will hear him. John testified of me. And the works I am performing testify. But you do not hearken to my message, nor hear the Father, nor accept John's message, and you ignore the evidence shown by my works. Therefore, you are deliberately blind and choose not to know my Father, because you have no faith in his truth and refuse to walk in his pathway.

9 You should carefully review again the scriptures, for you suppose they can save your soul, but they were written to testify of me. Although I can save your soul, you refuse salvation because you are opposed to me. I am not looking for vain popularity, but offer salvation for your souls. I understand what is in your hearts, and because you do not love God you do not love truth.

10 I have come to you because the Father sent me, and I glorify his name, but you reject that. If someone not sent by the Father comes to glorify himself by displaying his own wisdom, you respect him. How can you ever gain light and truth when you use one another as the final authority on truth, and ignore the light sent by the Most High God? I will not need to condemn you before the Father because Moses will do that. If you really believed Moses you would understand he prophesied and testified of me. Since you have perverted what Moses wrote, how can you hope to believe me?

11 After these events, Jesus went over the Sea of Galilee, which was renamed the Sea of Tiberias. And a large group followed him because they saw his miracles healing the injured and diseased. Jesus climbed up a mountain and there he taught his companions. And the feast was approaching. When Jesus noticed the throng approaching them, he asked Philip, Where can we buy bread to feed these approaching people? He asked Philip the question, but already planned what he was going to do. Philip answered him, Two hundred days' wages would not buy enough bread to even give each of them a little. Another companion, Andrew, Simon Peter's brother, said to him, There is a boy with us who has five barley loaves and two dried salted fish, which is obviously not enough to feed this crowd. Jesus said, Have the people sit down on the plentiful grass. About five thousand were seated. Jesus stood and looked up to Heaven, holding up the barley loaves. While blessing the loaves, he thanked his Father. Then he distributed food to his companions, and then passed through the multitude and gave to

each of them their fill of barley bread and salted fish. When the multitude were filled, Jesus asked his disciples, Gather every thing that remains uneaten so nothing is wasted. When it had all been gathered, the remainder filled twelve baskets, many times what had started with, five barley loaves and two fish. Then some of the multitude fed by this miracle testified, This is surely fulfillment of the sign of the Messiah, God's King and Priest, who will restore Israel as a nation!

12 When Jesus overheard that they wanted to force him to be their king, he walked away, going back up the mountain alone. That evening when some of the throng were leaving, his companions departed in a boat across the sea toward Capernaum. It was after dark and Jesus was not with them in the boat. At the time the sea became turbulent because of a strong wind. So when they had rowed about four miles, they saw Jesus walking upon the sea and approaching their boat; they were afraid. But he said, I am that I am, do not be frightened. They recognized this was another promised sign to identify the Messiah, and understood the meaning of his greeting, and then they were at their destiny.

13 The next day, when the throng left behind on the other side of the sea discussed leaving, they realized there was no other boat than the one his companions had used. They knew that Jesus had not been with them on the boat. They saw his companions leave without him. But he was now gone away also. And so, when other boats arrived from Tiberias near to where they were fed barley bread after the Messiah had blessed it, they took the available boats and went to Capernaum to try to locate Jesus. When they found him on the other side of the sea, they asked, Teacher, from what source did you come? Jesus replied, In the name of Father Ahman I tell you, You follow after me, not because you intend to obey what I teach, nor because you witnessed miracles and believe, but you are slaves to your bellies and want to be fed more barley bread. Do not be preoccupied with food for your bellies, but for food from God, that is, light and truth, leading to endless progression upward. I am Son Ahman and can give you sustaining light and truth, for God the Father has declared I am His Son.

14 Then they asked him, What do we need to do to enter God's pathway of endless progress? Jesus answered and said, The pathway is before you in me, I teach and display what the Father wants

you to witness and believe. They said in response, What sign will you give to us to confirm this pathway, so we can trust your message? What will you give to us? Our fathers were fed with manna in the desert for forty years. As the scripture states, He gave them bread from Heaven to eat. Feed us likewise.

15 Then Jesus said to them, In the name of Father Ahman I tell you the truth, Moses was not the one who gave bread, it was my Father who did that. But now my Father is offering true life-giving bread from Heaven, which is light and truth. For the Bread of God is sent from the Heavenly Council to give light and truth to the world. They responded, Master, feed us with this bread forever.

16 Jesus said bluntly to them, I am the bread that gives life; he that follows the path with me will never hunger for light; and any who believe on me shall never thirst for truth. Unfortunately, as I have already told you, even though you have seen me, you do not believe me. But my Father has provided some who will heed my words, and those who follow me I will safely keep. I am descended from above as a Messenger sent to follow Father Ahman's plan. Father's plan is that by completing my ascent I will have the power to rescue creation, losing nothing. Moreover, those who are here on this journey with me will be added upon for evermore if they have faith in me. They will rise up to likewise generate endless lives, worlds without end.

17 The Jews loudly objected to his claim of calling himself, I am, and equating himself with God, and because he claimed to be the bread which came down from Heaven. And they challenged his teaching, asking the people, Is not this Jesus, the son of Joseph, whose father and mother we know? How can he claim to descend from Heaven?

18 Jesus responded to them, Do not dispute my teaching between yourselves. No man can come unto me except he follows the path of my Father, who has sent me as His messenger of salvation. And this is what my Father expects of you, that you heed his Son. For the Father testifies he sent me, and anyone who accepts the Father's testimony, and has the faith in him to heed his testimony, I will raise upward in the resurrection of the just. For it is written in the prophets, And these shall all be taught by God. Every person who has hearkened and has learned the will of the Father, accepts

me as his messenger. None of you have seen the Father unless you first descended from God's presence, as I have come; and all who have seen the Father can testify of him. In the name of Father Ahman I declare to you, He that has faith on me has endless lives, worlds without end. I am that bread of life. This is the bread that descended from Heaven, that a man may eat of me and his life never end. Your fathers did eat manna in the wilderness and they perished. But I am the living bread sent from Heaven to rescue you. If any man takes into themselves this bread, he will gain light and truth and the power for endless life. The staff of life I provide is to sacrifice my flesh, which I will surrender to rescue the world.

19 The Jews argued among themselves, demanding, How can this man give us his flesh to eat? Then Jesus said to them, In the name of Father Ahman I say unto you, Unless you eat the flesh of the Son of Man, and drink his blood, you will never have endless life in you. Those who eat my flesh, and drink my blood, will obtain endless life. I will raise him up in the resurrection of the just at the last day. Just as the Father provided this life for me, I will provide it for you if you have faith in me. For my flesh will fill you with light, and my blood will quench you with truth. If you receive these, I will fill you with light and truth and we will be brothers, sons of God. My sacrifice is the bread I descended from Heaven to provide, not like the manna eaten by your deceased ancestors who rejected greater light and truth in their day. The light and truth I offer leads to endless lives, worlds without end.

20 The foregoing is what he taught in the Capernaum synagogue.

Chapter 6

Many of his followers, after they had heard him teach this in the synagogue, concluded, This is hard to accept; who can agree with it? When Jesus understood that even his close companions balked at it, he said to them, Are you offended by that? How are you going to have the faith to witness my ascent back to the Throne of the Father where I have come from? I have spoken of the Spirit of light and truth that enlightens. The flesh is nothing, and my message is about light and truth. My teachings are Spirit, and they are life. But there are some of you that do not understand because you do not believe. For Jesus knew from the beginning the ones who were faithless and foresaw who would betray him. And he said, Because of faithlessness I tell you that no faithless man can come with me. Only those who heed the will of my Father who sent me will have power to rise with me.

2 At that time many followers left and ended their journey with him. Then Jesus asked the twelve, Are you also going to leave? To which Simon Peter answered, Lord, where else is there to go? You teach the words of Eternal life. All of us believe and are certain that you are the Messiah, the Holy One of the Most High God. Jesus told them, Have I not chosen you twelve, and even among you one follows the accuser? He spoke of Judas Iscariot, the son of Simon, for he was one of the twelve and would ultimately betray him.

3 After this upheaval among his followers, Jesus taught in Galilee, but he avoided Judea because the Jews viewed him as a threat to their authority and were conspiring to murder him. Now the Feast of Tabernacles was about to begin. His half-brothers expected him to attend the feast and mentioned to him, Let us leave here and go to Judea, that your followers there can witness your good works. Because nobody hides from the public and can expect to be noticed. If you are going to work wonders, you really should show yourself in Jerusalem. But these half-brothers did not really believe in him. Then Jesus responded, My time of sacrifice is not yet come, but you are always ready to criticize. The world does not hate you, but it does hate me because I proclaim against false religion and hypocrisy. You go to the feast without me. I am not going with you. The time has not arrived for my life to end. After that conversation, he went as if he were returning to Galilee.

4 But after his half-brothers departed for Jerusalem, he turned and also headed for the feast, but traveled so as to be unnoticed. As was their practice, the Jews were on watch for him during the feast and were asking, Is he here? Have you seen him? Jesus was discussed by many people, debating whether he was a good man or a deceiver. But pilgrims avoided discussing him openly because they were afraid of the Jewish leaders who detested him.

5 During the celebration of the feast, Jesus arrived and openly taught in the temple courtyard. Hearing what he taught, the Jewish leaders were surprised and posed the question, How can he understand these complex things so well when he never received learning from us? Jesus responded to their question, My doctrine does not come from me, but from God who sent me. Anyone who walks in God's path will understand his doctrine, because that path increases light and knowledge. I testify of that path. Follow it and you will know whether I am sent by God or I am not sent by God. Teachers who preach from their own understanding only gratify their pride, but a teacher of truth teaches only what God tells him, and that teacher provides a light worth heeding.

6 Did not Moses give you commandments to follow, but you disobey them? How can you conspire to murder me when Moses' commandments forbid murder? The leaders defended themselves by responding, You are possessed by a lying devil. Who do you falsely claim is conspiring to murder you? Jesus replied to them, I did God's work and healed a man, and you were offended. Moses approved the practice of circumcision (it did not originate with Moses, but originated with the first Patriarchs at the beginning), but Moses continued the practice and you perform circumcision on the Sabbath. If you approve circumcising a man on the Sabbath day in order to obey the commandment of Moses, how can you disapprove of me healing a man on the Sabbath day, an act that makes him whole? Do not use your false traditions to decide if something is good, but use the light of God to decide if any action I take is approved by him.

7 Then some of the residents of Jerusalem came upon this exchange and inquired, Is not this the man the leaders want to kill? How is he teaching so boldly while they fail to silence him? Are the leaders afraid that he really is the Messiah? And others said, No, he is from Galilee. The Messiah obviously will not come from there,

but from Heaven. Jesus was in the temple as he taught, and he responded to these inquiries by saying, You are familiar with me, and you know I am from Galilee, but I have been sent by the Most High God and you refuse to acknowledge him. I know him. I am from him, and he has sent me. When they heard this, they wanted to kill him on the spot, but because the time for his sacrifice had not come they were held back. But there were those present who heard what he taught, and saw what he did, and believed, saying, When the Messiah comes, will he provide more evidence that he is sent by the Most High God than this man has provided?

8 The Pharisees overheard the comments of these believers, and they directed their guards to detain Jesus. But when the guards came, Jesus said to them, I will only be here for a little while, and then I will return to him who sent me. You will then want me to be with you, but at that time you will be disappointed. I will rise up to where you can never come. Then the leaders mocked his response, How can he rise up to a place we cannot go? Will he travel among the scattered Israelites to trouble them? Or try to make gentile converts? What foolishness he utters by claiming he can rise up where we can never come. We would not want to be with him. If he leaves us, why would we ever try to again be with him?

9 During the last day of the feast, Jesus proclaimed to the throng, If any man thirsts, let him come to me and drink. Anyone who believes on me, as the scripture promises, out of his belly shall flow rivers of living water (he was speaking of the Holy Spirit, which believers were promised. Following Jesus' resurrection, Divine Wisdom was promised to fill believers).

10 This produced controversy with some saying, He is certainly the prophet who Moses said we must heed or be cut off. Others said, He is the Messiah. But others said, He is not true because prophecy never stated the Messiah will come from Galilee. Does not the prophecy predict the Messiah will be a descendant of David and be from Bethlehem? The people were divided because of him. And some of them wanted to arrest him, but no one laid hands on him.

11 At a meeting of the Sanhedrin the guards were asked, Why have you not detained him and brought him to us? The officers answered, We have never heard any man speak like he does. Then members of the Sanhedrin said, Are you also deceived? Have any of

us who are members of the Sanhedrin believed on him? Only the
ignorant public, who do not keep the law as we do, are misled to
believe him. Nicodemus, who had earlier come to speak with Jesus,
asked, Does our law condemn a man before he can defend himself
or respond to the accusations against him? They asked him, Are
you also from Galilee? Search and look. There is no prophet foretold to come from Galilee. Their debate ended with that and
everyone went home.

12 Jesus spent that night on the Mount of Olives. Early in the morning he returned to the temple. A crowd gathered to hear him teach,
and he sat down and taught them. Jesus again testified to them, I
am the light of the world; he that follows me will not walk in
darkness, but shall be guided by the light of life.

13 The Pharisees challenged him by interrupting, You testify of
yourself. The law requires two witnesses and therefore your testimony cannot be true. Jesus replied to them, Even though I testify
of myself, my testimony is nevertheless true and binding, for I
know where I came from and where I am going, but you do not
understand where I came from nor where I am going. You debate
about geography rather than understanding that I come from God
who sent me. For the present I withhold from condemning you
leaders. But if I were to condemn you, I would be right to do so.

14 As for your claim that I am my only witness, I am not alone, but
the Father is also my witness. It is true the law you claim to follow
requires two witnesses. I am one, and the Father who sent me also
testifies as a witness of me. They asked him, Where is your Father?
Jesus answered, You do not know either me or my Father because if
you knew who I am you would understand who the Father is also.
He declared this while in the temple treasury as he taught in the
temple courtyard. The Sanhedrin failed to detain him because the
time for his sacrifice had not yet arrived.

15 Then Jesus repeated to them, I will continue onward following
the path of my Father, and you will not accompany me, but will
instead die under the burden of your sins. Therefore you cannot go
where I will be. Then the Sanhedrin scornfully asked, Does he plan
to kill himself? Is that why he said, The path he will take we will
not join? And Jesus responded to them, You are from a lower estate. I am from the Heavens. You are stuck in this world, and I am

not of this world. Because of this I said to you that you will die burdened with sins. If you do not believe that I am sent by the Most High God, bringing light and life with me, you will die burdened with sins. They said to him, So tell us who you claim to be. And Jesus answered them, I am the same as I told you from the beginning.

16 I have many things to teach that will be used to judge you; and the one who sent me is the Source of all truth. I am teaching what he has sent me to teach and he provided my message. They did not understand that he was speaking the words of Father Ahman. Then Jesus added, When you have lifted up the Son of Man, then you will realize that I am Son Ahman, and that I have done nothing on my own; but as my Father has taught me, I repeat his words. He sent me and accompanies me here; the Father has never abandoned my side. I always do the things that please him.

17 When he spoke these words, many believed on him.

18 Then Jesus addressed those Jews who believed on him, Only if you continue to follow my teachings will you be my students indeed, because you will know the truth, and the truth will make you free. The leaders interrupted to claim, We are Abraham's descendants, and have never been slaves to any man. Why do you say we will become free? Jesus answered them, In the name of Father Ahman I say unto you, Whoever misses the mark is the slave of errors. And such a slave will not be allowed to be within Abraham's house in the resurrection, but the Son will remain part of God's Family forever.

19 If the Son sets you free from sin, you are free indeed. I know that you are Abraham's descendants, but you conspire to kill me because my teachings have no place within you. I teach you what the Father has shown to me while I was in his presence, and you follow the teaching of your father. They answered and said to him, Abraham is our father. Jesus replied to them, If you were really Abraham's children, you would do the works of Abraham. But instead you plan to kill me. And why do you plan to kill me: I am a man that has only told you the truth that I have heard from the Most High God; Abraham would never do such a thing. You follow the example of your real father. Then they said to him, You are the product of extramarital fornication involving an unknown num-

ber of men, and we are not. We have one Father, even God. Jesus
said to them, If God were your Father, you would love me, for I am
sent by and represent God. I am not speaking my own words or
pursuing my own agenda, but the Father's words and agenda. Why
do you fail to comprehend my words? Your refusal to hearken and
submit to my teachings makes you deaf indeed. Your father is the
accuser, and you share the envy and rebellion of your father. He
was a rebellious destroyer from the beginning, and fought against
the truth, because he prefers lies. When he spreads a lie, he advances his agenda. He is the source of deceit in this fallen world.
And because I am the Source of truth, you are unable to believe me.
Which of you can truthfully show that I have missed the mark?
And if I teach the truth, why do you refuse to believe me? Everyone
who follows the Most High God hearkens to God's words. Because
you do not follow the Most High God, you cannot hear him.

20 Then the leaders retorted, When we refer to you as a Samaritan
possessed by a devil we have accurately described you. Jesus answered, I have no devil guiding me; I obey my Father, and you dishonor both him and me. I do not pursue acclaim or honor. You are
the ones that seek acclaim and wrongly judge me. In the name of
Father Ahman I say to you, If anyone stands watch awaiting direction from me, he shall not be overtaken even by death, throughout
eons. Then the leaders of the Jews said to him, Now we know that
you are possessed by a devil. Abraham is dead, along with the
prophets who were God's chosen. Yet you claim, If a man awaits
direction from you, he shall not be overtaken by death through the
eons. Do you claim you are greater than our father Abraham who
was overtaken by death, greater than the prophets who are dead? Is
there no limit to your vainglory? Jesus replied, If I honor myself,
my honor is nothing. It is my Father who honors me, the one who
you falsely claim is your God. Unlike me, you do not know him. If I
were to say, I do not know him, I would be as much of a liar as you
are when you falsely claim him as your God. I not only know him,
but I watch for his words like a sentinel always awaiting his direction. Your father Abraham rejoiced to see my day, and he saw it and
was glad. Then the leaders of the Jews mocked him saying, You are
not yet fifty years old, and yet you claim to have seen Abraham? Jesus said unto them, In the name of Father Ahman I say unto you,
Before Abraham was, he knew me as I am. Then they picked up
stones to throw at him because they regarded his statement as

blasphemy. But Jesus hid from their view and safely departed from the temple, bypassing the crowd undetected.

Chapter 7

And as Jesus departed Jerusalem, he saw a man who had been born blind. His followers inquired, Master, who sinned, this man or his parents, to cause him to be born blind? Jesus answered, Neither this man nor his parents caused this affliction, but his infirmity allows the mercy of God to be displayed by making him whole. I must perform the works of him that sent me while I am with you. The time is coming when I will have finished my work here, then I will return to the Father. As long as I am in the world, I am the giver of light in the world. When he said this he spat on the ground and made clay of the spittle. Then he anointed the eyes of the blind man with the clay and said to him, Go, wash in the pool of Siloam (which is by interpretation, Sent). The blind man left for the pool and washed, and he began to see.

2 The people who knew him and were aware of his blindness asked, Is not this the blind beggar? Some said, Yes it is him; others said, No he only resembles him, but the man said, I am he. Those who knew him asked, How did you obtain your sight? He answered and said, A man named Jesus made clay and anointed my eyes and said to me, Go to the pool of the Sent One and wash. I went and washed and I received sight. Then they asked him, Where is that man? He said, I do not know.

3 And they brought the formerly blind man to the Sanhedrin because once again Jesus healed the blind man on the Sabbath day. The leaders again asked the man the same question: How were you healed of blindness? He answered them, There was a man who put clay on my eyes, and I washed and was no longer blind.

4 Some of the Sanhedrin declared, That man cannot be of God because he breaks the commandment to never work on the Sabbath. But others said, How can a sinful man do such miracles? And there was a disagreement among them. They then asked the blind man again, Do you think the man who healed you was a sinner? He responded, He is a prophet.

5 But the leaders avoided settling the argument by deciding everything was a lie: Therefore the man had never been blind and did not have his sight restored. Then the parents of the man born

blind were asked, Is this your son who is claimed to have been born blind? How then does he now see? His parents answered, We know that this is our son and that he was born blind. But how he now has vision we do not know, nor do we know who cured his blindness. He is old enough to speak for himself so ask him, he should speak for himself. The parents were afraid of the leaders because the Sanhedrin had threatened to excommunicate anyone who claimed Jesus was the Messiah. This is why they said, He is old enough to speak for himself so ask him.

6 Then they threatened the man that had been blind telling him, Give God the praise; we know that this man is a sinner. He responded, Whether he is a sinner or not, I would not know. All I know is that I was blind, but now I can see. Then they asked him again, What did he do to heal you? How was he able to cause you to see? He answered them, I have told you already, and you do not believe. Will you believe if I repeat it and tell you again? And would that cause you to become one of his followers? Then they reviled him and said, You are his follower, but we follow Moses. We know that God spoke to Moses. As for this man we do not know where he comes from. The man answered and said to them, Why this is indeed a marvelous thing, that you do not know anything about the man, yet he has cured my blindness. But you teach that God does not listen to sinners, but if a man is obedient to God then God will answer his prayers. Since the world began, no man has restored eyesight to anyone born blind other than a prophet of God. If this man was not sent by God he could not have performed a miracle. The leaders reviled him by declaring, You were altogether born in sins, and are you attempting to teach us, who are not sinful? And they cast him out.

7 Jesus heard he had been cast out, and when he found him, he said to him, Do you believe on the Son of God? He replied, Who is he, Lord, that I might believe on him? And Jesus said to him, You have both seen him and spoken with him, and I am he. And the man said, Lord, I believe. And he knelt down and worshipped him.

8 Jesus said, I am here in the world to prove who is righteous and who is not. Those who have been blinded by falsehoods I can teach them to see, and for those claiming they see clearly, I will leave them in their blindness. And some of the leaders who were nearby overheard him say this, and asked him, Are we blind also? Jesus

said to them, If you were blind, you would not have sinned. But because you claim, We see, therefore your sins remain.

9 In the name of Father Ahman I tell you, If you do not enter by the doorway into the protective sheepfold, but climb in any other way, then you are only a thief and a robber. But when you enter at the door and the shepherd lets you enter, then you belong. The shepherd guards the entry, and his sheep respond to his voice. He calls his sheep by name and leads them up. He leads his sheep by his example and asks them to follow in his path, and they follow because they trust his words. His sheep will not follow another, but will flee from a stranger. They do not recognize the stranger's voice. Jesus told this parable to them, but they could not understand what he meant by the parable.

10 Then Jesus spoke to them again, In the name of Father Ahman I tell you, I am the door of the sheepfold. Every teacher now or before who has not testified of me are only thieves and robbers trying to take my sheep away, but my sheep have refused to heed them. I am the door. Any man who enters the sheepfold through me shall be saved and shall continue to progress and be supported. The thief only intends to steal, slay, and consume the sheep. I have come to preserve the lives of my sheep so that they might have abundant life.

11 I am the good shepherd, and a good shepherd will sacrifice his own life for the lives of his sheep. The true shepherd does not profit from the sheep, regarding them only as property, and cares nothing for the lives of the sheep. The false shepherd runs away when he sees a wolf approaching, letting the wolf destroy and scatter the sheep. I am the good shepherd and know my sheep, and they know me. But he who profits from the sheep flees, because he is only self-interested and cares nothing about the sheep. Just as the Father laid down his life for me, he trusts me with the lives of the sheep. I will sacrifice my life for the sheep.

12 I have other sheep that are not part of this fold. I will visit them and they will also hear my voice, and I will make all my sheep into one fold, following one shepherd. My Father loves and trusts me with the flock because I will sacrifice my life for them, and then take it up again to provide life for the flock. No one will take my life, but instead I will offer it as a willing sacrifice. I have made the

choice to lay it down, and I possess the power to take it up again. I received this commandment from my Father.

13 There was a debate among the leaders of the Jews because of Jesus' teachings. Most of them concluded that He has a devil in him, and it makes him a madman. They asked, Why listen to him? Others said, What he teaches are not the words of a devil or madman. Besides, would a devil restore sight to the blind?

14 Another confrontation happened at Jerusalem during the wintertime Feast of the Dedication. Jesus walked in the temple on Solomon's porch. The Jewish leaders came and surrounded him and said, How long do you intend to leave us guessing? If you are the Messiah, tell us plainly. Jesus answered them, I have already told you, and you did not believe. Consider the deeds I have accomplished in my Father Ahman's name, they identify me. But you will not believe even what you have seen me do, because you are not part of the flock given to me by the Father, as I have also told you before. My sheep respond to my voice, and I know them, and they follow me; and I cause them to have life. They shall never die throughout the eons, neither can any adversary remove them out of my hand. My Father, who gave them to me, is greater than all, and no adversary is able to take them out of my Father's hand. My Father and I are one.

15 Then the leaders of the Jews picked up stones again to execute him. Jesus rebuked them saying, Many good works have I showed you from my Father. For which of those acts are you going to stone me? The Jews answered him, We are not offended by good acts, but by your blasphemy which the law condemns with stoning. It is blasphemy for you, a man, to claim to be God. Jesus responded, Is it not written in the scriptures, I said you are gods? If God referred to those he spoke with as gods, and the scriptures are reliably true, how can you claim that I, who the Father sent as a witness of truth, commit blasphemy when I refer to myself as God's son? Judge me by what I do, and if I fail to do what God expects, then you do not need to believe me. But if I do what God tells me to do, even if you reject my words, consider my actions. They will convince you that God is within me, and I am within the Father. Whereupon they attempted again to detain him, but he escaped their hand and went away again beyond Jordan to the place where John first baptized. And he remained there. Many visited with him there. The visitors

heard him teach and remarked, John did no miracle, but every thing that John said about this man is true. Many were converted during the time he stayed there.

Chapter 8

Now a man named Lazarus, living in Bethany, who was the brother of Mary and Martha, was sick. It was in their house that Mary, the Elect Lady, anointed Jesus with sacred oil and cut his hair. Mary and Martha lived together in the Bethany house, and Lazarus was in their house while ill. The sisters sent a message to Jesus saying, Lord, have pity, our brother you love is gravely ill. And when Jesus heard of the sickness, he said, This sickness will not cause his death, but it will show the glory of God, and will make it clear that the Son of God is glorified by the Father.

2 Now Jesus loved the entire family, Martha, her sister, and Lazarus. Jesus waited two days after he heard Lazarus was sick, remaining where he was when first informed of the illness. After that delay he said to his followers, Now let us go to Judea again. But his disciples reminded him, Master, the Jews recently attempted to stone you; and you want to return there again? Jesus answered, Are there only twelve hours of light each day? During the daylight a man can see to walk and does not stumble and fall because the daylight informs him. But at night, without the light, a man stumbles because of the darkness surrounding him. He said these things, and he said also to them, Our friend Lazarus is now sleeping, but I will go to awaken him from his sleep. Then his disciples said, Lord, if he is sleeping he will be fine. However Jesus meant that he had died, but they thought he meant resting in sleep. Then Jesus said bluntly, Lazarus is dead. And I am glad for your sakes that I was not there, so that now you will believe; nevertheless let us go to him. Thomas, who is called Didymus, said to his fellow disciples, We may as well go with him so that we can die alongside him. They were all afraid the leaders of the Jews would arrest and kill Jesus, for they did not yet understand the power of God.

3 And when Jesus came to Martha's house in Bethany, Lazarus had already been in the grave four days. Now Bethany was near Jerusalem, less than two miles distant. There were many Jews at the house to mourn with Martha and Mary over their deceased brother. As soon as Martha heard that Jesus was coming and nearby, she hurried to meet him, but Mary remained in the house. Martha cried to Jesus, Lord, if you had been here my brother would not have died. But I know that even now whatever you ask of God,

God will give you. Jesus said to her, Your brother will rise again. Martha replied to him, I know that he will rise again in the resurrection at the last day. Jesus said to her, I am the resurrection, and the life. He that believes in me, even though he were dead, yet will he live. And whoever lives and believes in me will never die, worlds without end. Do you believe this? She said to him, Yes, Lord. I believe you are the Messiah, the Son of God, who was foretold to come into the world.

4 After this discussion, she quietly entered the house and told Mary to secretly leave with her. She said to her, Our Lord is here, and asking for you to meet with him. As soon as Mary heard that Jesus was there, she arose quickly and rushed out to meet him.

5 Jesus had not yet arrived in the town, but was still at the place where Martha met him. The Jews in the house who were mourning with her, saw Mary abruptly depart and thought she was overcome with grief and was headed to the grave. They said, She is headed to the grave to weep and mourn there. When Mary arrived where Jesus was, and saw him, she fell down at his feet and said to him, Lord, if you had been here, my brother would not have died.

6 Jesus looked upon her weeping, and the others who followed her also weeping, and he was grieved in his heart, and was troubled and said, Where have you laid his body? They told him, Lord, come and see. Jesus also wept. The Jews noticed and said, Look at how much he loved him! Some of them asked, Could not this man, who opened the eyes of the blind, have not also saved this man from dying? Hearing this Jesus again was grieved because of their misunderstanding.

7 And he went to the grave. It was a burial cave, and had a stone blocking entry to it. Jesus said, Remove the stone blocking the cavern. Martha, the sister of the deceased man, said to him, Lord, by this time his decomposing body will stink because he has been dead for four days. Jesus reminded her, Did I not tell you that if you would believe you would behold God's glorious power? Then they removed the stone blocking the cave where the body lay. Then Jesus looked up to Heaven and said, Father, I thank you that you have heard me. I know you always listen to me, but I mention it for the benefit of those who are here witnessing this moment. Perhaps they will believe that I have been sent by you if they hear my

prayer. Then with a loud voice Jesus commanded: Lazarus, return to us from the grave. The man who was dead came out from the grave, his hands and feet still bound by grave-clothes, and his face covered with a burial shroud. Jesus instructed them, Untie him, and let him go.

8 When the group of Jews who followed Mary saw what Jesus had done, most believed on him. But there were still some who immediately ran to the Pharisees to tell them what Jesus had just done.

9 When they heard the report, the leaders summoned the Sanhedrin to meet, discussing the event and asking, What should we do? This man continues to do many miracles. If we ignore him and this continues, everyone will believe him, and the Romans will respond by taking away our right to lead, and will break apart our followers. A participant named Caiaphas, who was the high priest at that time, said to them, You understand nothing about how to deal with this threat to ourselves. It is better for one man to die to save our people than for our people to be lost. These words were inspired by God. Because he was the high priest at the time, he unwittingly spoke a true prophecy that Jesus would die to save those people. He would not merely save the Jews but also God's people throughout the world, whom he would gather as his family. From that moment the leaders determined on a plan to have Jesus killed.

10 Jesus sensed their plan and avoided them. He traveled unseen into the Judean wilderness to the city of Ephraim, where he and his followers remained undetected.

11 The time for the Jewish Passover arrived. Many people traveled up to Jerusalem before the Passover to participate in ceremonies to purify themselves. The leaders looked for Jesus to be there and asked members of the crowd standing in the temple, What do you think, will Jesus be coming to the Passover? There was standing direction from the Sanhedrin that if anyone saw Jesus in the city they were to tell the informants so that they could detain him.

12 Six days before the Passover, Jesus returned to Bethany where he had raised Lazarus from the dead. They made supper for him and Martha served. Lazarus was among those who sat at the table with

him. Many came to be there to see the man who was raised from the dead and to hear Jesus who had raised him.

13 And among those who were present were his mother, and Mary, the Elect Lady who was companion with Jesus. She cut off the seven locks of his hair that had not been cut before because of the vow, which fell at her feet. This troubled his disciples who feared his strength would depart from him but said nothing because Jesus permitted it to be done. Jesus, seeing their concern, asked, Is not a lamb shorn before it is sacrificed? But they did not understand his meaning. And she took royal oil used to coronate a king, containing spikenard, frankincense and myrrh, and applied it to the head, arms and hands, legs and feet of Jesus. And the house was filled with the smell of the royal anointing oil. One of his disciples, Judas Iscariot, Simon's son, who would later betray him, spoke up and asked, Why was this anointing oil wasted instead of sold for a year's wages of $40,000, and the money used to help the poor? He did not say this because he cared for the poor, but because he was a greedy thief who acted as treasurer for the group, and he wanted to get control over the money. Jesus rebuked him and said, Leave her alone. My mother has safeguarded this gift from my birth until now to be used for this moment. This anointing is required to be done to establish me before I lay down my life. The poor are always in need in this world, but I reign among you for only a short while and then am offered up as a sacrifice on your behalf.

14 Many of the Jews heard he had come to this dinner and came to see not only Jesus, but also to see Lazarus who had been raised from the dead. The Sanhedrin wanted Lazarus killed also, because raising him from the dead converted many people to believe Jesus was the Messiah.

Chapter 9

On the following day, many of those who were there for the Passover heard that Jesus would be entering Jerusalem. They took palm tree branches and went out to greet him as he entered, and shouted, Hosanna! Blessed is the King of Israel that comes in the name of the Lord.

2 Jesus had sent two followers beforehand to get a young colt, and he entered Jerusalem riding on it. This was exactly what the prophet Zechariah foretold, Rejoice, daughter of Zion, shout out daughter of Jerusalem; behold, your King comes to you, he is just and provides salvation, meekly riding upon a young colt. At the time this happened, the disciples did not recognize that it was fulfilling prophecy, but after Jesus rose from the dead, then the disciples remembered the prophecy and how it had been fulfilled at that moment. The people who had been present when Lazarus was raised from the dead had spread word all over Jerusalem, and the welcoming crowd knew about that miracle and welcomed him into the city. The leaders were upset and said to each other, No one is following our direction. This whole population have become his followers!

3 In the crowd that gathered for the Passover, there were certain Greeks who went to Philip, who was from Bethsaida of Galilee, and asked him, Sir, would you introduce us to Jesus? Philip went to tell Andrew, and together they went to tell Jesus that people were eager to meet him. And Jesus responded, The time has arrived when the Son of Man will complete his journey. In the name of Father Ahman I tell you, except a kernel of wheat is buried in the ground, it remains but a seed, but if it is buried, it can spring to life and bear fruit. Those who love their life will lose it, but those willing to sacrifice their life in this world will obtain endless lives, worlds without end. If any man is loyal to me, let him follow me and every upward step I achieve, there will my loyal followers join me. Any who are loyal to me, my Father will approve.

4 Now I confront the final trial on my path, and what should I say? Father, save me from the difficulties I now face? When this is the reason I have come into the world. Father, let all honor be given to you. Then a voice from Heaven said, Every thing you have done has honored me, and every thing you will yet do will also honor me.

The people nearby also heard the voice, but some thought it was thunder. Others thought an angel spoke to him. Jesus explained, You did not hear this voice for my benefit, but you heard it for your benefit. The time has come for me to complete the work required of me, to intercede for the world. And the accuser will lose all his power. Because of the sacrifice of his life that the Son of Man is to make, he will rise up and rescue all mankind. He said this to explain how important his death was to save others. The people who heard this asked him, When we consult the scriptures they claim that the Messiah will live forever. Why do you say the Son of Man must sacrifice his life? Who are you talking about? Then Jesus said to them, Only a little time remains for the light who is now here. Learn how to live while the light remains, otherwise darkness will overcome you. Without the light you will fall into error. While you are near the light, believe in the light, so that you can become the children of light. Jesus said this, abruptly departed, and then avoided them.

5 Although he had done many miracles before them, they still did not comprehend that he was the Messiah, fulfilling the prophecy of Isaiah about the Messiah, Who has believed our report? For whose benefit has the strength of the Lord been revealed? And Isaiah answered those questions by describing them: They will refuse to believe because Isaiah wrote, Make the heart of these people grow fat, dull their ears and shut their eyes, so they will not see with their eyes and hear with their ears, and understand with their heart, and repent, and be healed. Isaiah saw the Messiah's glory and prophesied of him.

6 Despite conflicts, some of the Sanhedrin also secretly believed on him. But because of the Pharisees they did not admit their belief, fearing they would be ejected from the synagogue, for they valued the praise of men more than the praise of God.

7 Jesus declared, He that believes on me, believes not just on me, but also on the one who sent me. What you see me do is what he that sent me has done before. I am here as the light of the world to enable anyone who believes on me to escape from the darkness. I do not judge those who hear my words, but do not believe, because I did not enter the world to now judge it, but to be its savior. But when you reject my message, beware, because the message I was sent by the Father to deliver will separate you in the last day. He

will divide you based on your submission to, or rejection of, his message. He has sent me to guide you, and he guides into endless lives, worlds without end. My message, therefore, is the Father's.

Chapter 10

As the feast of the Passover approached, Jesus knew the time had arrived for his sacrificial death and return to the Father. He had loved and ministered to those who believed on him, and remained ministering to them until the end. At the conclusion of supper, Judas Iscariot, the son of Simon the leper, had been seduced by the accuser to betray Jesus.

2 Jesus knew the Father had empowered him to have dominion over all things because he had been sent by the Father to redeem the world, then to return to the Father once he departed from the world. And so Jesus arose from supper and removed his cloak and took a towel as an apron. And he poured water into a basin, and he began to wash the disciples' feet and to dry them with the towel he wore as an apron. When he came to Simon Peter, Peter objected, saying, Lord, why do you wash my feet? Jesus answered and said to him, You will not understand this now, but will later come to understand this ordinance is necessary. Peter said to him, You do not need to wash my feet. Jesus answered him, If I do not wash your feet then you cannot rise up to be with me, for it is a required ordinance to be with me. Simon Peter still did not understand and said to him, Lord, if you must then don't just wash my feet, but finish the ordinance also on my hands and head. Jesus replied, Those whose hands and head have been washed only need to receive washing of their feet, and are clean from the blood and sins of this world. You whom I have washed today are clean, but not all of you. Now the ceremonies of the Jews under their law required them to wash, but Jesus washed for a higher purpose. And he knew who would betray him. Therefore he said, Not all of you are clean.

3 So after he had washed their feet and replaced his cloak and sat down again, he said to them, Do you understand the example I have just provided to you? You call me Master and Lord. And that is correct to say, for I am. If I am your Lord and Master, and knelt to wash your feet to cleanse you, you should also labor to make each other clean from the blood and sins of the world. For I have given you the example that you should do as I have done with you.

4 In the name of Father Ahman I declare to you, No servant is greater than his Lord, nor am I who have been sent greater than my Father, who sent me. Since you know these things, you will

have joy if you follow them. I do not expect all of you to do as I have shown you. I know whom I have chosen, but the Psalm prophesies that my familiar and trusted friend, who ate bread with me, has lifted up his heel against me. I am telling you this beforehand so that when I am betrayed you do not lose your belief in me. I am the Messiah. In the name of Father Ahman I declare to you, He that accepts my word spoken by whomever I send with my word receives me, and he that receives me receives him that sent me, even my Father.

5 When Jesus said this, he was troubled in spirit and declared, In the name of Father Ahman I say to you, one of you will betray me. Then the disciples looked at one another, wondering who he was talking about. One of the disciples Jesus loved was next to him at the table. Simon Peter got his attention and asked him to inquire of Jesus who he was referring to as a traitor. That disciple next to Jesus then asked him quietly, Lord, who is going to betray you? Jesus answered, It is the one to whom I will hand the bread I now dip. And when he had dipped the bread, he gave it to Judas Iscariot, the son of Simon. And he took the bread, at which point the accuser took control of Judas. Then Jesus said to him, What you have planned, do it quickly. Now no one at the table understood why he said this to him. For some of them thought that because Judas was the treasurer, Jesus was saying to him, Buy the things needed for the coming meal, or perhaps, he should give something to the poor. Judas, having received the bread, left immediately and entered the darkness.

6 Then, after Judas had departed from them, Jesus said, Now is the Son of Man glorified, and God is glorified in him. If God is glorified through his sacrifice, God shall also glorify the one sacrificing himself and will never abandon him. Little children, I will only be with you a little while yet. You will want me here, but remember I said to the Jews, I will go onward on my path, and you will not take it with me. Now I tell you the same thing.

7 I give you a new commandment, That you love one another. Love each other as I have loved you. If you have love for each other it will be a sign that will identify you to all mankind as my followers.

8 Simon Peter asked him, Lord, where are you going? Jesus answered him, The steps I take next on the path, you will not be tak-

ing for now, but you will take those steps later on as you travel the same path. Peter responded to him, Lord, why can I not follow you right now? I am willing to lay down my life for you. Jesus answered him, Will you lay down your life for me? In the name of Father Ahman I tell you, The rooster will not crow tomorrow morning before you have denied me three times.

9 Do not allow your heart to be troubled. You are devoted to God and are also devoted to me. In the journey through my Father's realms are many stages with temporary abodes. If it were not so, I would have told you. I go to prepare an abode for your upward journey. And when I arise, I will prepare places for you, but I will be your companion again and visit each of you, so that where I travel, you may journey to also. And the path I follow upward you know, and the way of ascent you also know. Thomas said to him, Lord, we don't know where you are going; how can we know the way? You have not told us. Jesus said to him, I am the way, the record of the truth, and the means for Eternal lives, worlds without end: no man comes to the Throne of the Father without me. If you follow me, you will come to the Father's Throne through me and will thereafter be like him forever.

10 Philip said to him, Lord, reveal to us the Father and that will be all we ask. Jesus responded to him, Have I been with you this long and you still do not yet know who I am, Philip? Any who see me has seen my Father. How can you ask, Reveal to us the Father? Do you understand that I am in the Father, and the Father is in me? Do you understand that the words that I speak to you came from the Father, who is one with me? Nothing I have done is mine. Understand that the Father, who is one with me, is to be given credit for all I have done or will do. Believe me that I am one with the Father, and the Father is one with me; but if you do not, at least believe through these works. In the name of Father Ahman I declare to you, the individual who trusts me, what I have accomplished he will also. Followers will also accomplish the greater works I do next. Followers will also finish the path, as I am now concluding, at the place my Father dwells. As he helps me, I will help you, and you will accomplish what I have along with the greater sacrifice I have yet to finish. And whatever you shall ask in my name, I will answer, so that the Father may be glorified by the honor shown his Son. If you shall ask any thing in my name, I will answer.

¹¹ If you love me, stand ready, watching for every communication I will send to you. Remember that I will ask the Father, and he will provide to you another Comforter, that he may be by your side endlessly. You will obtain the record of Heaven, the truth of all things which is denied to the world because the world refuses my Father, and therefore they do not know him. But you know him, for he is with you, and shall provide answers to guide you. I will not leave you comfortless. I will stand at your side also.

¹² Yet a little while, and the world will no longer see me, but you will not lose sight of me because I give life, and you shall share in endless lives. You will know that I and the Father are one, and I am one with you, and you are one with me. He that treasures my teachings, and stands ready, watching for every communication I send him, is he who shows love for me. To those who show love for me, my Father will show love to them, and I love all those, and I will personally minister to them.

¹³ Judas (not Iscariot), asked, Lord, how is it you will manifest yourself to us, but not to the world? Jesus answered and said to him, If a man loves me, he will stand ready, watching for every communication I will send to him; and my Father will also love him, and we will come visit him, and continually abide by his side.

¹⁴ Whoever claims to love me but does not stand ready, watching for every communication I will send, indeed does not love me. These teachings are not from me, but come from the Father who sent me.

¹⁵ These words have I spoken to you while I am still present with you. But the Comforter, which is the Holy Ghost that the Father will send in my name, will teach you all things, and restore to your memory all truth I have taught to you, and the record of Heaven itself.

¹⁶ I leave you in peace, the peace only my teachings can provide for you and not as the world claims to find peace. Do not be confused nor fearful. You heard me say to you, I am leaving, and will return again. If you loved me, you would be rejoicing because I told you I am returning to my Father's realm. My Father dwells in the highest Heaven. I foretell you about what remains for me to accomplish so that you are not confused as it happens. When the coming

events unfold I will not be able to explain it further as it occurs. The prince of darkness will not overcome me, but he can overcome you if you are confused and fearful. Remember, I explained that I will suffer because of my love for the Father, and he requires me to pass through this ordeal for your sakes, and I am ready to comply. Now let us walk together from this place.

¹⁷ I am the true vine or head of the Father's family, and my Father is the husbandman over that family. Every branch connected to me that does not produce fruit, he will remove, and every branch that produces fruit he will prune back so that it produces better fruit. You will bear fruit if you follow the things I have taught you. Stay connected to me as part of the Heavenly family, and I will nourish you. Just as a branch cannot produce fruit if it is not connected to the vine, neither will you be able to bear fruit unless you remain connected with me. I am the vine, and you are the branches. He that stays connected to me, and I to him, will be abundantly fruitful; but without the connection to me you will perish. If a man loses his connection with me, he is merely a withered branch; and men take the withered branches, cut them away and burn them. If you stay connected to me, and my words live in you, you will ask according to my will, and you will be given the ability to accomplish my will. It will please and vindicate my Father if you produce abundant fruit, and that will prove you follow me. Just like the Father has loved me, I have in turn likewise loved you. Therefore, remain connected with me and my love will be with you. If you practice my teachings you will always remain connected with me; just as I have kept my Father's teachings and have remained connected with him.

¹⁸ I say these things to you so I will be able to rejoice at your triumph. You will overcome all obstacles if you follow what I have taught.

¹⁹ This is my commandment: That you love one another as I have loved you. No man loves more than when he is willing to sacrifice his life to save his friends. You are my friends if you do whatever I communicate to you. Beginning now, I will no longer call you my servants because a servant does not share his Lord's life. But I make you my friends because every thing I received from my Father I have shared and will yet share with you. You did not choose me, but I have chosen you, and ordained you, that you should progress

and become fruitful, that your fruit will testify on your behalf forever, that whatever I direct you to seek from my Father you will be able to obtain. I have taught these things to you to enable you to share my love among one another.

20 The world will hate you, but you know that it hated me before it hates you. If you belonged to the world, the world would love its property. But because you are not a captive of the world, and I have freed you from the world, the world hates you.

21 Remember that I told you before that no servant is greater than his Lord. If many have persecuted me, many will also persecute you, but if some few have followed my teachings, some few will follow yours also. The world's response to you will be because you will act in my name and on my behalf. Those who fight against you are strangers to my Father. If I had not come and testified of the truth to them, they would not be accountable for rebellion, but now they have no excuse for their rebellion. If they hate me, they hate my Father also. If I had not shown to them an example no other man has shown before, they would not be accountable. But they have rebelled after seeing with their own eyes and hearing with their ears the one sent by Father Ahman to them, and have rebelled against us both. Proving men in this way fulfills the prophecy, They hated me without a cause.

22 As for you, when the Comforter comes (or in other words the Spirit of truth emanating from my Father), that spirit will testify of me. Then you have the ability to also testify of me. This is because you have followed me from the beginning or before the world was organized.

23 Now I tell you beforehand what to expect to come upon you so you are not surprised, nor will you stumble and fall. They will excommunicate you. The time will even come that the self-righteous who kill you will think that they speak for God. And they will do these things because they cannot do what the Father and I have done. I warn you beforehand that you will face this opposition so that when it happens you will remember and be strengthened. When I first taught, the anger and opposition was directed at me, and because of that, you were not their focus. But now I will return to the one who sent me and they will turn their anger at you.

24 I said that I return to the one who sent me and none of you asked me to explain what I meant by that. Instead you have become saddened and downhearted. Understand this truth from me: It is for your benefit that I ascend to the Father. If I do not take up my position there I cannot send the spirit of truth, the record of Heaven, the peaceable things of immortal glory to lead you upward. Once I ascend to the Father, I will send the Comforter to guide you on the upward path. The light is given to shine upon the pathway, to expose wrongdoing, and let you decide matters correctly. Those who refused to become devoted to me will not receive this. Because I will ascend to the Father, you will be guided, and they who follow the adversary will be rejected with the adversary they follow. He has already been rejected by the Father.

25 There are many things I still have to teach you, but you are not able to understand it all as yet. When I am the Spirit of Truth, I can then reveal to you the record of Heaven and knowledge will be poured into you. The spirit is the means to communicate my words, and my words will lead you on the upward path. The knowledge poured in to you will come from me. I will depart, but only briefly because when I ascend back to the Head of the Household of Heaven, I will also be by your side to guide you by my voice from Heaven.

26 Then some of his disciples questioned among themselves, What does he mean he will depart briefly, then when he has ascended to the Father he will be by our side? What do these words mean? We do not understand.

27 Now Jesus knew that they wanted to ask him to explain and said to them, Do you discuss among yourselves what I meant when I said, I will depart, but only briefly, because when I ascend back to the Father, I will be by your side to guide you by my voice from Heaven? In the name of Father Ahman I forewarn you, You will grieve and mourn, but that will turn to joy and rejoicing. When a woman is in labor she suffers because the time to give birth has come, but after the child is born she forgets the pain and is joyful over her newborn child. You will mourn my departure, and celebrate my return, and that joy will never leave you. Then you will not need to ask of me, but you should ask Father Ahman in my name for what is needed. From now on, inquire from Father Ahman using my name and you will always receive an answer.

²⁸ Much of what I have said to you may seem like a riddle, but the time will come when you will comprehend my words and they will no longer seem a riddle, and you will understand them plainly. When I ascend and you ask the Father in my name, you will know that Father Ahman loves you because you have been devoted to me, and have accepted that I came from the Head of the Household of Heaven and was sent by him into the world, and that I will return to be with him.

²⁹ His disciples said unto him, Very good, now you are making it clear and not using a riddle. We are certain that you did come from the Father and were sent by him. Jesus answered them, At this moment you are truly committed in this belief, but the time is quickly upon us when you will scatter in fear and leave me alone to face the adversary. Even without you I will never be alone, because the Father remains with me in every trial here. I tell you this beforehand so you will be reassured. In this world there are difficult trials to be faced by my followers, but those who remain devoted will, like me, finish the path and experience the fullness of joy.

³⁰ Then Jesus looked up to Heaven and said these words, Father, the hour has arrived. Let your light abide with your Son, that your Son may be filled by your light and illuminate others. Because you have taught me to overcome the weaknesses of the flesh, you guide me to gain power to heal all weaknesses and redeem all creation. From your presence come Eternal lives, worlds without end, and you are the sole source of all truth. Therefore, it is known and will be known that I am the Messiah sent by you. I have kept every obligation you have asked of me and now have completed this part of the work. Let what happens next finish your great work, so I may return to your Throne to be with you where I was before my descent here.

³¹ I have explained your title to the men you gave to me from out of the fallen creation. They were yours at the beginning, and you have given them to me as my offspring. And they are devoted, prepared and always waiting to respond to your words. Now they understand and accept that every thing I have done and taught comes from you. For I have said to them the things you told to me. They are devoted to the truth and know I am your sent Messiah. I pray for them, and what I ask is for them and not the world, for they are yours. And all who are devoted to me are yours, and you share with

me, and I am their light. I am soon to depart from this creation, but these followers will remain here as I return again to be with you. Holy Father, please watch over these like a sentinel. Protect and guard them using your power, so that they may be united as one, as we are united as one. While I accompanied them in the world, I shared light with them in your name. Every one you gave to me I have kept, and none of them will be lost to us, other than the son of perdition. Those who are kept and those who are lost are divided according to your covenant made from the beginning.

32 And now I will be returning to you, and I declare these words in the world so these devoted believers can share in my coming joyful triumph. I have taught them your word, and the world rejects them because they are not taken in by worldliness, even as I am not distracted by the world. I do not ask for you to remove them from the coming challenges here, but protect them from falling prey to temptations of worldliness. They are not worldly, even as I am not. Sanctify them through your truth. Your words are truth. As you have sent me into the world, likewise I am sending them into the world. And for their sakes I sacrifice myself, that they might be sanctified through the truth.

33 I pray not only for these followers, but also for all believers who learn our words from them. I ask that all followers and believers may be united as one, as you, Father, are in me, and I am in you, that they also may be united as one in us. By them becoming one, the world will have reason to believe that you sent me. And the light which you gave to me I have given to them. This allows them to become united as one, even as we are one: my light in them, and your light in me. The light will lead them to be made perfect in one. That light I have given to them is evidence to the world that you have sent me. I have loved them, as you have loved me. Father, I ask that those whom you have given to me may also ascend to live where I am ascending, for this journey was established before the foundation of creation. O righteous Father, this fallen world does not know you, but I have declared that you have sent me to minister here. I have declared your message here and will finish the course. May the love you have for me be shown through the example of my love for them, and they may be saved through my sacrifice.

Chapter 11

When Jesus had spoken these words, he took his disciples and walked across the Cedron brook, where there was a garden that he and his disciples entered. And there he worked wondrously, his disciples being overcome with awe, collapsed to the ground.

2 Jesus had often visited this garden, and Judas knew of the place. Judas led a party under orders by the Sanhedrin, carrying lanterns, torches and weapons. Jesus knew what would happen, and confronted the armed party asking, Who are you looking for? They answered, Jesus of Nazareth. He declared, I am that I am! Hearing this bold claim startled the Sanhedrin's armed men, and they tripped over one another when they took a surprised step backwards. Jesus asked again, Who are you looking for? (to require them to acknowledge by their own voice that he was the God of Israel). And they said, Jesus of Nazareth. Jesus answered, I have told you that I am!

3 Jesus said, If you are looking for me, then let these others go on their way. This request was to fulfill his prophecy, Every one you gave to me I have kept, and none of them will be lost to us.

4 Then Simon Peter had a sword and drew it, and struck the high priest's servant and cut off his right ear. The servant's name was Malchus, who later believed on Jesus. Then Jesus said to Peter, Put your sword back in the sheath. The cup my Father has given to me, should I refuse to drink it?

5 Then the party under orders from the Sanhedrin took Jesus, and bound him. And they led him away first to Annas, the father-in-law of Caiaphas, who was the high priest during that year. Now Caiaphas was the same man who counseled that it is better for one man to die to save the people than for the people to be lost.

6 Simon Peter followed behind Jesus, and so did a second disciple who was familiar to the high priest and was permitted access to enter the high priest's house. But Peter remained outside by the door. After entry, the second disciple returned and spoke to the doorkeeper and gained access for Peter to enter the house also. The doorkeeper asked Peter, Aren't you one of the accused man's fol-

lowers? He answered, No I am not. And there were members of the party who brought Jesus back who were warming themselves beside a coal fire, and Peter was also cold so he warmed himself beside them.

7 The high priest questioned Jesus about the identities of his followers and about his doctrine. And Jesus answered him, I spoke boldly to everyone. I taught frequently in the synagogue and in the temple, where the Jews are present to hear. I have made no attempt to be secret. Why ask me these questions? Ask the many people who heard me teach and they can tell you what I said; they know. After he said this, one of the men holding Jesus hit him with his palm and said, Do you dare to speak to the high priest that way? Jesus responded to him, If I have spoken like an evil sorcerer, testify of the sorcery, but if not, why did you strike me? Annas then had him taken in the bindings and brought to Caiaphas, the high priest.

8 As Simon Peter stood and warmed himself, the people standing by the fire asked him, Are you not one of his followers? He denied it, and said, No I am not. One of the servants of the high priest who was related to the man whose ear Peter had cut off then asked, Did I not see you in the garden with him? Peter then denied again, and immediately the crowing of a rooster sounded.

9 Then they led Jesus from Caiaphas to the Roman judgment hall, and it was still before sunrise. The Sanhedrin did not enter the judgment hall because it would defile them and prevent them from participating in the Passover. Pilate came out and confronted them and asked, What accusation do you have against this man? They answered and said to him, Would we bring him to you if he were not a sorcerer? Then Pilate said to them, That is no Roman concern. You take him, and judge him against your own law. The Jews therefore said to him, We do not crucify a man on the Passover under our tradition, referring to the prophecy Jesus had spoken about the kind of execution he would suffer.

10 Then Pilate stepped back into the judgment hall and addressed Jesus and said to him, You are the King of the Jews? Jesus answered him, Did you say this to me on your own, or did others tell you to say it to me? Pilate answered, Am I a Jew? Your own people and the chief priests have turned you over to me. How do you justify your-

self? Jesus answered, My kingdom is not of this world. If my kingdom were of this world, then my followers would fight to prevent
the Jews from taking me as their captive. But my kingdom is not
comprised of the Jews. Pilate responded, So you admit you claim to
be a King? Jesus replied, It was you that just said I was a king. The
reason I was sent into this world was to be a witness of the truth.
Every person who is loyal to the truth listens to my teachings. Pilate responded to him, What is truth? And after saying this, he
went out again to the Jews and said to them, I find no reason to
punish him. You have asked me for clemency for a Jewish prisoner
to respect your Passover; shall I free your King of the Jews? They all
shouted out, Not this man, but Barabbas. Now Barabbas was a
robber.

11 Then Pilate had his guards take Jesus and beat him. And the soldiers put on his head a crown of acanthus, and they dressed him in
a purple robe and said, Hail, King of the Jews! and they hit him
and made sport of him. Pilate thereafter went back out, and said to
the Jewish leaders, Behold, I bring him back to you, that you may
know that I find no reason to punish him any further. Then Jesus
came out wearing the crown of acanthus and the purple robe. And
Pilate said to them, Behold the man!

12 When the chief priests and leaders saw him, they cried out saying, Crucify him! Crucify him! Pilate said to them, You take him
and you crucify him, for I have no quarrel against him. The Jews
answered him, We have a law, and our law imposes the death
penalty because he blasphemed by falsely claiming to be the Son of
God.

13 When Pilate heard them say that, he was alarmed, and he returned with Jesus into the judgment hall and asked him, Who are
you? But Jesus did not answer. Then Pilate said to him, Do you
refuse to speak to me? Do you not realize that I have the power of
life and death? Jesus answered, You have no authority over me except that permitted by Heaven. Those who handed me over to you
have the greatest sin. Pilate decided then that he would release
him of any charge, but the Jews shouted, If you let this man go you
are not loyal to Caesar. When anyone claims to be a king he commits treason against Caesar. When Pilate heard that accusation, he
brought Jesus out and sat down in the judgment seat in a place
called the Pavement; in Hebrew called Gabbatha. At the time it was

approaching mid-day, time to begin to prepare the Passover feast. Pilate announced to the Jews, Behold your King! But they shouted back, Take him away and crucify him. Pilate said to them, Shall I crucify your King? The Jewish leaders declared, We have no king but Caesar. We will crucify him ourselves. And Pilate turned him over to those who were going to crucify him, sending but one soldier to accompany them with a plaque he ordered to be displayed.

14 And they took Jesus, and led him away. And he carried his cross and was taken to a place called the place of the skull, which had the Hebrew name Golgotha. Here the leaders directed his crucifixion, and two others who had been crucified by the Romans were also there at the same time, one on either side, with Jesus in the middle. When Pilate surrendered Jesus to be crucified, he had a plaque prepared in Hebrew, Greek and Latin to be displayed on the cross. The plaque announced: Jesus of Nazareth the King of the Jews. This announcement was read by many of the passing Jews. For the place where Jesus was crucified was beside the city road and many pilgrims were walking by. Then the chief priests of the Jews complained to Pilate, Either take it down or do not write: The King of the Jews. Instead write that he claimed, I am King of the Jews. Pilate answered, That which I have written I have written.

15 Now the guards, when they had crucified Jesus, took his garments and made four parts, to every guard a part; and also his coat. The coat was without seam, woven from the top throughout. They agreed among themselves, Let us not cut it up, but cast lots for it, and someone will take it whole. This fulfilled the prophecy in scripture that foretold, They parted my raiment among them, and for my vesture they did cast lots. This prophecy foretold how the guards would divide his raiment as he was dying.

16 Now remaining at the cross with Jesus were his mother, and his aunt, and Mary the wife of Cleophas, and Mary the Elect Lady. When Jesus saw his mother and the beloved disciple standing together, he said to his mother, Woman, behold your son! Then he said to the disciple, Behold your mother! And from that hour that disciple accepted her as part of his own household.

17 After this, Jesus knowing that every thing had been fully accomplished to fulfill prophecy said, I thirst. Now there was a vessel full of vinegar, mixed with gall. They dipped a sponge into it and using

a hyssop branch raised it to his mouth. When Jesus had received the vinegar, he said, My path is completed! Then he bowed his head and entrusted his spirit back to the Father.

18 The Jews were concerned about preparations for the Passover, and did not want crucifixions to continue into the Holy Day. Therefore they inquired of Pilate to find if he would object if they had the legs of the crucified broken to quickly bring about their death. Pilate agreed, and the Roman guards broke the legs of the two who were being crucified when Jesus was added. But when they approached Jesus, he was already dead, and therefore there was no need to break his legs. A soldier under Pilate's command used a spear to stab under the fifth rib, and blood and water exited the wound. The beloved disciple who was there saw this and testifies it happened, so you can trust this eyewitness account. The things that happened fulfilled the prophecy that foretold, A bone of him shall not be broken. And again another prophecy said, They shall look on him whom they pierced.

19 After his death, Joseph of Arimathea, a secret follower of Jesus who was afraid of the Jews, asked Pilate if he could take the body of Jesus. Pilate permitted him to take Jesus' body. He went, and Nicodemus (who had also visited Jesus in secret) accompanied him and brought a hundred pounds of myrrh mixed with aloes, used by Jews to cover bodies when buried. They covered the body with the mixture and wrapped it with linen to bury him. Near to the place where crucifixions were done, there was a garden. In that garden was a new sepulcher never before used. They laid the body of Jesus there because it was nearby, and the time for the holy feast was approaching.

Chapter 12

The first day of the week Mary the Elect Lady went in the early morning while it was still dark to the burial sepulcher. She saw the stone was rolled away from the sepulcher, and two angels sitting on it. Then she ran to Simon Peter, who was with the other disciple Jesus loved, and said to them, They have removed the Lord out of the sepulcher, and we do not know where he is now established. Peter and the other disciple departed for the sepulcher, running together. The other disciple outran Peter and arrived first at the sepulcher. And he bent down, and looked in, and saw the linen burial cloths. But he did not enter the tomb. Then Simon Peter joined him, and he went into the sepulcher and saw the linen burial cloths, and also the shroud that covered his body. It was not lying with the other burial cloths. Instead it was folded and set down alone. Then the other disciple who arrived first, also entered the sepulcher, and he saw the empty tomb and believed. They still did not understand the prophecy that he must rise again from the dead. Then the disciples departed to return home.

2 But Mary stood outside the sepulcher weeping. And as she wept, she bent down and looked into the sepulcher. She saw two angels in white, the one at the head, and the other at the feet where the body of Jesus had lain. They asked her, Woman, why are you mourning? She answered them, Because someone has removed the body of my Lord, and I do not know where he is now. After she said this, she walked away and then saw Jesus standing in the garden area. She failed to recognize that it was Jesus. Jesus asked her, Woman, why are you mourning? Who are you looking for? She assumed he was tending the garden, and answered, Sir, if you have taken him away, tell me where he is, and I will claim him. Jesus said to her, Mary.

3 She raised her face, recognized him, and addressed him, Greatest of Teachers, which is to say, My Lord. They embraced and Jesus told her, You cannot hold me here. I need to ascend right now to my Father. Go to my followers and say to them, I ascend to my Father and your Father, and to my God and your God.

4 Mary the Elect Lady came and told the disciples that she had seen the Lord, and that He had spoken these things to her.

5 Later on that same first day of the week, in the evening, when the doors of the room in which the disciples were meeting were closed and locked because of their fear of the Sanhedrin, Jesus came and stood in the middle of this group, and said to them, Peace be with you. And when He said this, He showed to them His hands and His side to prove it was He. Then the disciples were overjoyed, as they beheld their Lord. Jesus repeated to them, Peace be with you. As My Father has sent Me, even so I send you. And after He said this, He breathed upon them, and said to them, I convey to you the Holy Ghost. Whoever's sins you remit, they are remitted to them; and whoever's sins you retain, they are retained.

6 But Thomas called Didymus, one of the twelve, was absent when Jesus visited them. The other disciples relayed to him, We have seen the Lord. But he responded, Except I also see in his hands the print of the nails, and put my finger into the print of the nails, and thrust my hand into his side, I will not believe. And eight days after this, His disciples were in the same room again, and Thomas with them. Again the doors were locked, and again Jesus came and stood in the middle, and said, Peace be with you. Then He said to Thomas, Reach out your finger and touch my hands. Reach out your hand and feel my injured side. Do not be faithless, but be believing. And Thomas answered and said unto Him, My Lord and my God! Jesus said to him, Thomas, because you have seen me, you believe. Blessed are they that have not seen, and yet believe.

7 And there were many other signs that His disciples witnessed that testified of Jesus, but which are not contained in this account. But what is recorded is to testify that Jesus is the Messiah, the Son of God, so that you may obtain Eternal lives, worlds without end through His name.

8 I am the one who has testified in this account. And after the many other testimonies of Him, this is my testimony most recent of them all: I saw his glory that He was in the beginning before the world was. Therefore, in the beginning the Word was, for He was the Word, even the messenger of salvation – The light and the Redeemer of the world, the Spirit of truth, who came into the world because the world was made by Him, and in Him was the life of men and the light of men. The worlds were made by Him. Men were made by Him. All things were made by Him, and through Him, and of Him.

9 And I, John, bear record that: I beheld His glory, as the glory of the Only Begotten of the Father. He was full of grace and truth, even the Spirit of truth. He came and dwelt in the flesh, and lived among us.

10 And I, John, saw that He received not of the fullness at the first, but received grace for grace. And He received not of the fullness at first, but continued from grace to grace, until He received a fullness. And in this way He qualified to be called to become the Son of God, because He received not of the fullness at the first.

11 And I, John, bear record, and lo the Heavens were opened, and the Holy Ghost descended upon Him in the form of a dove and remained upon Him. There came a voice out of Heaven saying: You are my Beloved Son, this day I have begotten you; for I was there with John the Baptist when he baptized Jesus.

12 And I, John, bear record that He received a fullness of the glory of the Father. And He received all power, both in Heaven and on earth, and the glory of the Father was with Him, for he dwelt in Him.

13 The Father testified of Jesus also on the Mount, when He was transfigured before us, and the glory of Heaven was upon Him, and we saw Him enter the Heavenly realm. The Father testified also when our Lord prayed for those who do follow Him. And the Holy Ghost has and does testify of Him to all who receive Him. Therefore, we know by irrefutable evidence that Jesus is the Messiah, sent to fulfill prophecy, and to lead all who will follow through the path of His Father.

14 After this Jesus showed Himself again to the disciples at the Sea of Tiberias. This is an account of that event: There were together Simon Peter, and Thomas called Didymus, and Nathanael from the city of Cana in Galilee, and the sons of Zebedee, and two others, also disciples. Simon Peter said to them, I ascend to the deep. They responded to him, We go with you. They went forth, and entered into the ark; and they could not grasp anything.

15 But at the horizon of the morning star, Jesus stood at the sacred entry; however the disciples could not recognize it was Jesus for the glory about Him. Then Jesus asked them, Children, have you

celebrated the ritual meal? They answered Him, No. And He directed them and said, Approach the veil to the east and you will find what you seek. They approached the veil as instructed, and now they were overcome by the multitude of what was received. Therefore the disciple Jesus loved said to Peter, It is the Lord. Now when Simon Peter heard that it was the Lord, he quickly clothed himself (for he did not wear the apparel), and cast himself into the great deep. And the other disciples came into the ark and parted also the veil (for they were not bound by the limits of this world).

16 As they ascended, they saw a fire burning at the offering place and the Flesh Offering was upon it, who is also the Bread of Life. Jesus said to them, Rise above the flesh you now occupy, and Simon Peter ascended, and drew the veil open, and there were ministering a hundred, and then fifty, and then three; and for these many who they beheld, yet the veil remained open.

17 Jesus said to them, Come and eat the food of the rising sun. And none of the disciples asked of him, What name is now yours? knowing that it was their Lord. Jesus then served to them His flesh and blood, and they were filled by His Spirit. This was now the third time Jesus ministered to His disciples following His rise from among the dead.

18 After the meal, Jesus said to Simon Peter, Simon, son of Jonas, do you love me above every thing else? He answered him, Yes, Lord. You know that I love you. He said to him, Take care of my lambs as they are growing. He asked him again the second time, Simon, son of Jonas, do you love me above every thing else? He said to Him, Yes, Lord you know that I love you. He said to him, Take care of my lambs as they increase. He said to him the third time, Simon, son of Jonas, do you love me above every thing else? Peter was concerned because He asked him for a third time, Do you love me? And he said to Him, Lord, you know all things. You know that I love you. Jesus said to him, Care for my lambs as they are added upon. In the name of Father Ahman I tell you, when you were progressing, you dressed yourself, and went where you chose to go; but as you approach the end of the path, you will have to let others stretch out your hands and likewise nail you, even if you plead to have the bitter cup removed. This He said to foretell the sacrificial death that is required for endless glory. And then He added, You must follow after me.

¹⁹ Then Peter turned and looked at the disciple whom Jesus loved, who was behind. This was him who was next to Jesus at supper, and had quietly asked Him during supper, Lord, who is the one that will betray you? Peter saw him and asked Jesus, Lord, and what will become of this man? Jesus explained, I said to him, John, my beloved what do you desire? And John replied, Lord, give to me the power that I may bring souls to you. And I said to him, In the name of Father Ahman I commit to you that because you desire this you shall tarry until I return in my glory.

²⁰ And for this reason the Lord said to Peter, if I will that he tarry till I come, what is that to you? For he desires from me that he might bring souls to me, but you desire that you might come to me in my kingdom. I tell you, Peter, yours was a good desire, but my beloved has undertaken a greater work on earth. In the name of Father Ahman I say to you that you shall both have what you requested, and you both will have joy from what you each requested.

²¹ Now, therefore, know that Jesus is the Messiah, the Walker in the Path who has proven for evermore that Father Ahman sent Him into the world to prove His Father's path.

²² In addition to this account, many other things were done by Jesus, which, if they were all written, that library would fill the entire cosmos. Amen.

COMPARATIVE STUDY

What follows is a side-by-side harmonized comparison of the Testimony of St. John as found in the Restoration Edition (RE) of the Scriptures, juxtaposed with the traditional King James Version (KJV) of the Gospel according to St. John. It is hoped that with careful study, this format will reveal to the astute reader many insightful and enlightening differences between these two versions of John's record that can be discovered in no other way.

RE Chapter 1

KJV Chapter 1

¹In the Highest Council of Heaven there was One who spoke out. And the One who spoke out was among the Gods, and He was a God. He was in the Council of the Gods, and the creation of the cosmos was organized through Him. And without Him does not exist one thing that has come into existence in the cosmos. In Him was the power of life and this power was conveyed into the cosmos as the Light in men and every thing. The Light shone in the chaos and those in darkness have not been able to grasp it.

²There was a man sent from God and his name was John. This man was sent as a witness so that he might testify and identify the Light to give everyone a reason to believe through the Messiah. He, John, was not the Light, but he was sent by Heaven as a witness to testify of the Light, and to end the dispensation of Moses, and baptize to begin a new dispensation. The Light enlightens every man who is progressing upward in the cosmos.

³The Messenger of the Heavenly Council was in the cosmos, and the cosmos existed through Him, and the cosmos had not acquired His knowledge. He came into His own creation, but those there were unable to understand Him. As many as perceived the Light in Him, to them He gave knowledge to enable them to follow the path to become like Him, begotten children in the family of the Most High God. This is only possible for those who be-

¹In the beginning was the Word, and the Word was with God, and the Word was God. ²The same was in the beginning with God. ³All things were made by him; and without him was not any thing made that was made. ⁴In him was life; and the life was the light of men. ⁵And the light shineth in darkness; and the darkness comprehended it not.

⁶There was a man sent from God, whose name was John. ⁷The same came for a witness, to bear witness of the Light, that all men through him might believe. ⁸He was not that Light, but was sent to bear witness of that Light. ⁹That was the true Light, which lighteth every man that cometh into the world.

¹⁰He was in the world, and the world was made by him, and the world knew him not. ¹¹He came unto his own, and his own received him not. ¹²But as many as received him, to them gave he power to become the sons of God, even to them that believe on his name: ¹³Which were born, not of blood, nor of the will of the flesh, nor of the will of man, but of God. ¹⁴And the Word was made flesh, and dwelt among us, (and we beheld

lieve through His name. Those who believe through His name are no longer born of blood to follow the appetites of flesh, nor the ambitions of man, but are able to become, like Him, the offspring of God. This one who was Spokesman from the Heavenly Council was made flesh, and He temporarily cast His tent among us, and we could see His knowledge of the path to ascend in light and truth, he was a member of the Family of God, full of the power to ascend and able to display truth to others.

4John bore witness of him, and proclaimed, This is He of whom I testified; He who would be born after me has advanced in progression above me. He has advanced in progression far beyond everyone else in this sphere. For in the Council of Heaven was the Spokesman, even God's Heir, who is born into the flesh and sent to us to fulfill the will of the Father. And as many as obtain authority in His name shall gain the right to ascend to Heaven. We who have witnessed His fullness comprehend what Eternal life means through Him revealing the pathway of ascension to the Throne of God. For the law was given through Moses, but life and truth come through Jesus the Messiah. The law gave carnal instructions, but led only to condemnation and death. The gospel is to empower endless life, through Jesus the Messiah, the Only Begotten Son, who is a manifestation of the love of the Father. No man has seen the Father without hearing Him testify of the Son, for only through Him is any soul saved.

his glory, the glory as of the only begotten of the Father,) full of grace and truth.

15John bare witness of him, and cried, saying, This was he of whom I spake, He that cometh after me is preferred before me: for he was before me. 16And of his fulness have all we received, and grace for grace. 17For the law was given by Moses, but grace and truth came by Jesus Christ. 18No man hath seen God at any time; the only begotten Son, which is in the bosom of the Father, he hath declared him.

5And this was the witness of John, when the Jews sent priests and Levites from Jerusalem to inquire, Who are you? And he did not deny that he possessed the Spirit of God's messenger, but declared, I am not the Messiah. And they asked him, How then do you possess the Spirit of God's messenger? And he said, I am not that messenger foretold to come and restore all things.

6And they asked him, Are you the prophet Moses said God would raise up from among Israel, like unto Moses, in whose mouth God would put His words and he shall speak all that God commands him? And it will come to pass that whosoever does not hearken to that prophet, God will judge. Do you claim to be that prophet? And he answered, No.

7Then they asked, Who then are you? We are obligated to convey your answer to them that sent us. What do you say for yourself? He said, I am a voice of one crying in the wilderness, Make straight the way of the Lord, as predicted would be sent by the prophet Isaiah.

8And the inquirers who were Pharisees asked him, Why then are you baptizing if you are not the Messiah, nor come as the messenger to restore all things, nor the prophet foretold by Moses to whom we must give heed? John answered, I baptize with water, but there is one standing among you, whom you do not acknowledge and I bear testimony of him. He is the one foretold by Moses, and he will

19And this is the record of John, when the Jews sent priests and Levites from Jerusalem to ask him, Who art thou? 20And he confessed, and denied not; but confessed, I am not the Christ. 21 And they asked him, What then? Art thou Elias? And he saith, I am not. Art thou that prophet? And he answered, No.

22Then said they unto him, Who art thou? that we may give an answer to them that sent us. What sayest thou of thyself? 23He said, I am the voice of one crying in the wilderness, Make straight the way of the Lord, as said the prophet Esaias.

24And they which were sent were of the Pharisees. 25And they asked him, and said unto him, Why baptizest thou then, if thou be not that Christ, nor Elias, neither that prophet? 26John answered them, saying, I baptize with water: but there standeth one among you, whom ye know not; 27He it is, who coming after me is preferred before me, whose shoe's latchet I am not worthy to unloose.

preach following my witness of him. He has progressed beyond me so much that in comparison I am not worthy to kneel before him; his shoe's latchet I am not worthy to unloose, nor am I worthy to wash his feet. I could never substitute for him. He will baptize, not only with water, but also with fire and with the Holy Ghost.

9The next day John beheld Jesus coming to him, and said to those who were with him, Behold the Sacrificial Lamb of God, who will redeem from the fall of the creation! And John testified of him to the others, saying, This is him I described before, saying, After me will come a man who has progressed far beyond me, for he existed before me in Heaven. I recognize him, and testify to Israel that he is that Prophet foretold by Moses to whom all must give heed. Therefore I am here baptizing with water to prepare people for him.

29The next day John seeth Jesus coming unto him, and saith, Behold the Lamb of God, which taketh away the sin of the world. 30This is he of whom I said, After me cometh a man which is preferred before me: for he was before me. 31And I knew him not: but that he should be made manifest to Israel, therefore am I come baptizing with water.

10And John recounted, When I baptized him, I saw the Spirit descending from Heaven in a sign of a dove, and it abode upon him. I recognized him as God's Son because God, who sent me, and commanded me to baptize to prepare people to hear him, told me, On the man you see the Spirit descend in a sign of a dove and remain with him, he will be the one sent to bestow the Holy Ghost. I saw this happen, and testify that he is the Son of God.

32 And John bare record, saying, I saw the Spirit descending from heaven like a dove, and it abode upon him. 33And I knew him not: but he that sent me to baptize with water, the same said unto me, Upon whom thou shalt see the Spirit descending, and remaining on him, the same is he which baptizeth with the Holy Ghost. 34And I saw, and bare record that this is the Son of God.

11The foregoing events happened in Bethabara beyond Jordan, as John baptized there.

28These things were done in Bethabara beyond Jordan, where John was baptizing.

¹²On the next day after, John stood beside two of his followers, and noticing Jesus as he walked nearby, he said to the two others, Behold the Sacrificial Lamb of God! And these two who had followed John, when they heard that testimony, followed after Jesus. Then Jesus turned, and saw them following him, and asked, What do you want? They called him, Rabbi (which means acknowledged teacher), and asked, How can we understand the truth and advance? He replied, All men move upward by gaining light. If you advance you will learn to be like me. And these two went with him and were taught, and were his companions through that day, for it was mid-afternoon. One of the two who heard the testimony of John and followed Jesus was Andrew, Simon Peter's brother. That evening he went to his brother Simon and said to him, We have found the Messiah! And he brought Peter to Jesus. And when Jesus beheld him, he said, You are Simon, the son of Jonah. You will be called Cephas, which is, by interpretation, a seer, or a stone. And these men were fishermen, but they immediately left every thing else behind to follow Jesus.

¹³The day following Jesus went to Galilee, and encountered Philip, and said to him, Follow me. Now Philip was at Bethsaida, the residence also of Andrew and Peter. Philip found Nathanael and said to him, We have found the Prophet that Moses foretold in the law, and who the prophets promised would come, Jesus of Nazareth, the son of Joseph.

³⁵Again the next day after John stood, and two of his disciples; ³⁶And looking upon Jesus as he walked, he saith, Behold the Lamb of God! ³⁷And the two disciples heard him speak, and they followed Jesus. ³⁸Then Jesus turned, and saw them following, and saith unto them, What seek ye? They said unto him, Rabbi, (which is to say, being interpreted, Master,) where dwellest thou? ³⁹He saith unto them, Come and see. They came and saw where he dwelt, and abode with him that day: for it was about the tenth hour. ⁴⁰One of the two which heard John speak, and followed him, was Andrew, Simon Peter's brother. ⁴¹He first findeth his own brother Simon, and saith unto him, We have found the Messias, which is, being interpreted, the Christ. ⁴²And he brought him to Jesus. And when Jesus beheld him, he said, Thou art Simon the son of Jona: thou shalt be called Cephas, which is by interpretation, A stone.

⁴³The day following Jesus would go forth into Galilee, and findeth Philip, and saith unto him, Follow me. ⁴⁴Now Philip was of Bethsaida, the city of Andrew and Peter. ⁴⁵Philip findeth Nathanael, and saith unto him, We have found him, of whom Moses in the law, and the prophets, did write, Jesus of Nazareth, the son of Joseph.

14And Nathanael asked him, Can the promised Messiah come from Nazareth? Philip said to him, Come and see. Jesus saw Nathanael coming to meet him, and said of him, Behold a pure Israelite indeed, in whom is no guile! Nathanael asked him, How do you know anything about me? Jesus answered him, Before Philip called you, when you were praying under the fig tree, I heard your prayer. Nathanael responded, Rabbi, you must be the Son of God. You are the King of Israel. Jesus responded to him, You believe in me because I said to you that I heard your prayer under the fig tree? You will see greater things than these. And he said to him, In the name of Father Ahman I promise you, Hereafter you shall see the fiery ascent to Heaven open, and the angels of God ascending and descending to visit the Son of Man.

46And Nathanael said unto him, Can there any good thing come out of Nazareth? Philip saith unto him, Come and see. 47Jesus saw Nathanael coming to him, and saith of him, Behold an Israelite indeed, in whom is no guile! 48Nathanael saith unto him, Whence knowest thou me? Jesus answered and said unto him, Before that Philip called thee, when thou wast under the fig tree, I saw thee. 49Nathanael answered and saith unto him, Rabbi, thou art the Son of God; thou art the King of Israel. 50Jesus answered and said unto him, Because I said unto thee, I saw thee under the fig tree, believest thou? thou shalt see greater things than these. 51And he saith unto him, Verily, verily, I say unto you, Hereafter ye shall see heaven open, and the angels of God ascending and descending upon the Son of man.

KJV Chapter 2

15On the third day of the week, there was a marriage in Cana of Galilee; and the mother of Jesus was there. Jesus and his followers were invited guests at the marriage. And when the wedding party wanted more wine, his mother said to him, They have run out of wine. Jesus replied, Mother, why are you talking to me about it? The time for me to provide sacramental wine has not yet arrived. But his mother instructed the servants, Whatever he tells you to do, follow through with it.

1And the third day there was a marriage in Cana of Galilee; and the mother of Jesus was there: 2And both Jesus was called, and his disciples, to the marriage. 3And when they wanted wine, the mother of Jesus saith unto him, They have no wine. 4Jesus saith unto her, Woman, what have I to do with thee? mine hour is not yet come. 5His mother saith unto the servants, Whatsoever he saith unto you, do it.

16There were six waterpots made of stone that were used for ceremonial purification in religious obser-

6And there were set there six waterpots of stone, after the manner of the purifying of the Jews, con-

vances, each containing twenty to thirty gallons. Jesus instructed the servants, Fill the waterpots with water. And they filled them up to the brim. And he said, Now remove some and take it to the host. And they took it to him. When the host of the wedding tasted the ceremonial water, it had been converted to wine. But he did not know the source that converted the water, unlike the servants who recognized the Source. The host of the feast called for the bridegroom, and praised him using a proverb, saying, Careful men introduce their plans using the best wine, and later, when their followers are drunk, then their worst — but you have brought us better wine than at the start.

17This was a sign confirming his role as the Messiah that was performed by Jesus in Cana of Galilee. It was a demonstration of authority over both the elements and ordinances of salvation. Those who recognized this as a sign of his authority were awed as they considered it was him present among them.

18After this he went down to Capernaum, he, his mother, his brothers, and his disciples, and they were there a few days. As the Passover arrived, Jesus traveled up to Jerusalem where in the temple, there were appointed traders selling oxen, sheep, and doves, and others exchanged coins to profit from the temple donations. Seeing this, Jesus made a whip using small cords, and he drove the profiteers out of the temple, and also their sheep and oxen; and dumped

taining two or three firkins apiece. 7Jesus saith unto them, Fill the waterpots with water. And they filled them up to the brim. 8And he saith unto them, Draw out now, and bear unto the governor of the feast. And they bare it. 9When the ruler of the feast had tasted the water that was made wine, and knew not whence it was: (but the servants which drew the water knew;) the governor of the feast called the bridegroom, 10And saith unto him, Every man at the beginning doth set forth good wine; and when men have well drunk, then that which is worse: but thou hast kept the good wine until now.

11This beginning of miracles did Jesus in Cana of Galilee, and manifested forth his glory; and his disciples believed on him.

12After this he went down to Capernaum, he, and his mother, and his brethren, and his disciples: and they continued there not many days. 13And the Jews' passover was at hand, and Jesus went up to Jerusalem, 14And found in the temple those that sold oxen and sheep and doves, and the changers of money sitting: 15And when he had made a scourge of small cords, he drove them all out of the temple, and the sheep, and the oxen; and poured out the changers'

out the exchangers' money, and turned over the tables; and confronted those who were profiteering from Passover, saying, Get your business out of here and do not degrade my Father's house to merely your place of business. It reminded his disciples of the Psalm, The zeal of thy house hath eaten me up.

¹⁹The temple authorities, who had authorized the profiteering, confronted Jesus asking, If you think you have a right to exercise authority over the temple, while identifying yourself as God's son, show us a sign to prove you have this right, so we can believe you. Jesus answered and said, I will replace the holy of holies in three days with a new holy House of God. The Jews declared, It took forty-six years to build this temple, and will you replace it in three days? But he was talking of the temple of his resurrected body. Later after he was resurrected from the dead, his disciples remembered he had said this to the temple authorities, and they remembered the scripture, and what Jesus had said to the disciples.

²⁰Now while he was in Jerusalem at the Passover many believed on his name when they saw the healing miracles he did. But Jesus did not attempt to have them pledge loyalty to him because he knew they were fickle, and miracles alone cannot produce faith, because sign-seekers are wicked and adulterous.

money, and overthrew the tables; ¹⁶And said unto them that sold doves, Take these things hence; make not my Father's house an house of merchandise. ¹⁷And his disciples remembered that it was written, The zeal of thine house hath eaten me up.

¹⁸Then answered the Jews and said unto him, What sign shewest thou unto us, seeing that thou doest these things? ¹⁹Jesus answered and said unto them, Destroy this temple, and in three days I will raise it up. ²⁰Then said the Jews, Forty and six years was this temple in building, and wilt thou rear it up in three days? ²¹But he spake of the temple of his body. ²²When therefore he was risen from the dead, his disciples remembered that he had said this unto them; and they believed the scripture, and the word which Jesus had said.

²³Now when he was in Jerusalem at the passover, in the feast day, many believed in his name, when they saw the miracles which he did. ²⁴But Jesus did not commit himself unto them, because he knew all men, ²⁵And needed not that any should testify of man: for he knew what was in man.

RE Chapter 2

1There was a Pharisee named Nicodemus, a member of the Sanhedrin, who was in darkness and came to visit with Jesus. He sought wisdom from Jesus and said, Enlightened heavenly guide, some of us know you have descended from the High Council of Heaven because signs confirm you have authority from God. Jesus answered and said to him, In the name of Father Ahman I testify there is a new dispensation begun. You must accept the ordinances of this new Light or you cannot hope to progress to know God.

2Nicodemus said to him, If I believe this, can I ascend in this life, or will it be accomplished only in the afterlife? Jesus answered, In the name of Father Ahman I say to you, Except you receive the ordinance of baptism to join the new dispensation, and thereby forsake your sins and receive forgiveness and an outpouring of the Spirit, you will not ascend to God's presence in this life or the life to come. All who are devoted to the ambitions of the flesh remain imprisoned by the flesh, and those who are born anew through the ordinances, receive the Spirit of Truth, and are able to know the record of Heaven by the Spirit of Truth. Do not question if what I say is true because the Spirit of Truth confers light, knowledge, and understanding of the mysteries of Heaven within every soul who receives it.

3Nicodemus replied to him, Why is this not widely known? Jesus answered, Why does a member of the

KJV Chapter 3

1There was a man of the Pharisees, named Nicodemus, a ruler of the Jews: 2The same came to Jesus by night, and said unto him, Rabbi, we know that thou art a teacher come from God: for no man can do these miracles that thou doest, except God be with him. 3Jesus answered and said unto him, Verily, verily, I say unto thee, Except a man be born again, he cannot see the kingdom of God.

4Nicodemus saith unto him, How can a man be born when he is old? can he enter the second time into his mother's womb, and be born? 5Jesus answered, Verily, verily, I say unto thee, Except a man be born of water and of the Spirit, he cannot enter into the kingdom of God. 6That which is born of the flesh is flesh; and that which is born of the Spirit is spirit. 7Marvel not that I said unto thee, Ye must be born again. 8The wind bloweth where it listeth, and thou hearest the sound thereof, but canst not tell whence it cometh, and whither it goeth: so is every one that is born of the Spirit.

9Nicodemus answered and said unto him, How can these things be? 10Jesus answered and said unto

Sanhedrin not recognize that a new dispensation has begun? In the name of Father Ahman I confirm what was told by John the Baptist and I have begun a work that comes from Heaven. But you who lead Israel fight against it and you refuse to humble yourselves. If I offered you a position of respect and authority, as you now hold, you would believe. But because I testify only of heavenly things that require faith and sacrifice, you refuse to believe? I tell you, if you want to ascend to the Heavenly Council, you must first acknowledge and give heed to the messengers sent by them. You can refuse to believe, but you will see in me a sign and remember this saying: When Moses nailed a brass serpent upon a pole in the wilderness, he prophesied of me. And I shall also be nailed upon a tree, and those who believe on me will receive deliverance through my sacrifice, even as Israel was delivered by looking with faith at Moses' serpent.

4Father Ahman loves the world, and like father Abraham, Father Ahman will allow His Son to become an offering for sin. Whoever believes and follows His Son will not be lost, but have everlasting life. For God did not send His Son into the world to condemn the world, but to save the world. Those who believe and follow His Son will escape the limitations of sin. The faithless are condemned already because they refuse to believe and obey the Only Begotten Son of God. Every thing about my assignment, which I am now performing, was foretold by the

him, Art thou a master of Israel, and knowest not these things? 11Verily, verily, I say unto thee, We speak that we do know, and testify that we have seen; and ye receive not our witness. 12If I have told you earthly things, and ye believe not, how shall ye believe, if I tell you of heavenly things? 13And no man hath ascended up to heaven, but he that came down from heaven, even the Son of man which is in heaven. 14And as Moses lifted up the serpent in the wilderness, even so must the Son of man be lifted up: 15That whosoever believeth in him should not perish, but have eternal life.

16For God so loved the world, that he gave his only begotten Son, that whosoever believeth in him should not perish, but have everlasting life. 17For God sent not his Son into the world to condemn the world; but that the world through him might be saved. 18He that believeth on him is not condemned: but he that believeth not is condemned already, because he hath not believed in the name of the only begotten Son of God. 19And this is the condemnation, that light is come into the world, and men loved darkness rather than light, because their deeds were evil. 20For every

prophets sent earlier to teach Israel, for they all testified of me. They told you I would come, and I am now here doing what was prophesied, but you refuse to see it happening. Enough is underway that rejecting it means you prefer darkness to light. Humble yourself and admit the prophets foretold the very things now underway; repent and be baptized and the Spirit of Truth will open your eyes. If you want greater light, you will obey this instruction. If you refuse, then you never meant it when you greeted me as an enlightened heavenly guide.

one that doeth evil hateth the light, neither cometh to the light, lest his deeds should be reproved. 21But he that doeth truth cometh to the light, that his deeds may be made manifest, that they are wrought in God.

RE Chapter 3

After this Jesus and his disciples went to the land of Judea, and while there he taught, dined and worshipped with, and baptized them. John the Baptist was also baptizing north of there in Aenon, near to Salim, where the water was plentiful at that time of year. Crowds continued to go to John, and this occurred before he was imprisoned.

22After these things came Jesus and his disciples into the land of Judæa; and there he tarried with them, and baptized. 23And John also was baptizing in Ænon near to Salim, because there was much water there: and they came, and were baptized. 24For John was not yet cast into prison.

2 A controversy arose between traditionalist Jews and John's followers about authority to baptize. The traditionalists hoped to have John denounce Jesus baptizing. They went to John, hoping to turn his answer against Jesus. They asked John, The man you baptized beyond Jordan now is also baptizing and drawing away people to follow him, but he has not been given authority by us or by you.

25Then there arose a question between some of John's disciples and the Jews about purifying. 26And they came unto John, and said unto him, Rabbi, he that was with thee beyond Jordan, to whom thou barest witness, behold, the same baptizeth, and all men come to him.

3 John answered and said, Authority comes from Heaven, to both him

27 John answered and said, A man can receive nothing, except it be

and to me. I told you I am not the Messiah, but I have been sent to prepare the way for the Messiah. I am only like a guest at another man's wedding, and not the groom. But I rejoice to be in the groom's company. Jesus is the groom. He is the one whose mission is the more important. He must increase, but I must decrease. I have come to end an era in Israel, but he has come to begin another. He descended from Heaven to serve here, and all of us need to acknowledge him – I not only refuse to deny his authority, I confirm it.

4 Because John the Baptist saw and heard Jesus identified by Heaven as the Messiah, he testified boldly of him. But few people were willing to accept John's testimony about Jesus. Despite that, his testimony was true. God made John a witness and therefore John's witness was binding. Jesus was a messenger sent from the Heavenly Council to declare the truth, and Jesus had limitless access to the record of Heaven, the truth of all things, the light that quickens every thing. He is the one Moses prophesied would come and all Israel must give him heed or be cut off. God the Father loves and acknowledges Jesus as His Son, and has made him the steward over all creation. We are required to acknowledge God's Son to be rescued by him, for only the Son can rescue us from the Fall of Adam. Jesus lived as the example, proving the pattern for redemption from the Fall as he progressed from grace to grace, until he received a fullness, or in other words, grew in light

given him from heaven. 28Ye yourselves bear me witness, that I said, I am not the Christ, but that I am sent before him. 29He that hath the bride is the bridegroom: but the friend of the bridegroom, which standeth and heareth him, rejoiceth greatly because of the bridegroom's voice: this my joy therefore is fulfilled. 30He must increase, but I must decrease. 31He that cometh from above is above all: he that is of the earth is earthly, and speaketh of the earth: he that cometh from heaven is above all.

32And what he hath seen and heard, that he testifieth; and no man receiveth his testimony. 33He that hath received his testimony hath set to his seal that God is true. 34For he whom God hath sent speaketh the words of God: for God giveth not the Spirit by measure unto him. 35The Father loveth the Son, and hath given all things into his hand. 36He that believeth on the Son hath everlasting life: and he that believeth not the Son shall not see life; but the wrath of God abideth on him.

and truth until he was filled with truth and stands as the light of the world.

5 When the Pharisees learned that Jesus made and baptized more disciples than John, and that John's popularity could not be turned against Jesus, they conspired about how to have both John and Jesus executed. Some of the Pharisees thought John might be a prophet, but none of them believed on Jesus, whom they rejected and did not respect. Jesus recognized this was how they viewed him.

6 Unlike John the Baptist, Jesus baptized only a few people, instead preferring that his followers perform the rite and learn to minister. When he left Judea to return to Galilee, he informed his followers that he was required to visit Samaria on the way.

KJV Chapter 4

1When therefore the Lord knew how the Pharisees had heard that Jesus made and baptized more disciples than John,

2(Though Jesus himself baptized not, but his disciples,) 3He left Judæa, and departed again into Galilee. 4And he must needs go through Samaria.

RE Chapter 4

1He next went to the city of Shechem in Samaria, at the foot of Mt. Gerizim, adjacent to the parcel of ground which Joseph inherited from his father Jacob, which is the place where Jacob's well was located. Jesus was tired from the journey, it being about midday, and he sat down on the wall of the well. A woman of Samaria came to draw water. Jesus asked her, Could you give to me a drink?

2His followers were not with him, but had left to buy food in the city and therefore he was alone. The Samaritan woman replied to him, I do not understand why a Jew would ask me as a Samaritan to

5 Then cometh he to a city of Samaria, which is called Sychar, near to the parcel of ground that Jacob gave to his son Joseph. 6Now Jacob's well was there. Jesus therefore, being wearied with his journey, sat thus on the well: and it was about the sixth hour. 7There cometh a woman of Samaria to draw water: Jesus saith unto her, Give me to drink.

8(For his disciples were gone away unto the city to buy meat.) 9Then saith the woman of Samaria unto him, How is it that thou, being a Jew, askest drink of me, which am a woman of Samaria? for the Jews

give you a drink. Jews look down on us as unclean, so why would you ask me such a thing?

3Jesus replied, I have been sent by God, and if you recognized who now asks you to give a drink of water, you would gladly do so and ask me in turn for the gift of living water. The woman responded to him, Sir, you have nothing to reach the water, and the well is deep, so how can you suggest you could offer living water? Are you greater than our father Jacob, to whom God gave this well, who drank here with his children, and he watered his cattle from this source? Jesus answered her, Whoever drinks water from this well will thirst again, but whoever drinks from the living water which I shall give him shall live from eternity to eternity, for the Source in me will be the power to rise upward forever, worlds without end.

4The woman said unto him, Sir, give me of the water that I no longer will thirst nor need to come here to draw from this well. Jesus said unto her, Go, get your husband and I will teach you together. The woman replied, I have no husband (she spoke of herself). Jesus said to her, You are right, even though you have had five husbands (he meant this of both her and also the Samaritans whose Israelite blood was mixed with five other nations), and the man you live with presently has not married you (meaning both her and her province). So you are correct saying you have no husband. The woman said unto him, Sir, you speak like you are a prophet. Our fathers, the

have no dealings with the Samaritans.

10Jesus answered and said unto her, If thou knewest the gift of God, and who it is that saith to thee, Give me to drink; thou wouldest have asked of him, and he would have given thee living water. 11The woman saith unto him, Sir, thou hast nothing to draw with, and the well is deep: from whence then hast thou that living water? 12Art thou greater than our father Jacob, which gave us the well, and drank thereof himself, and his children, and his cattle? 13Jesus answered and said unto her, Whosoever drinketh of this water shall thirst again: 14But whosoever drinketh of the water that I shall give him shall never thirst; but the water that I shall give him shall be in him a well of water springing up into everlasting life.

15The woman saith unto him, Sir, give me this water, that I thirst not, neither come hither to draw. 16Jesus saith unto her, Go, call thy husband, and come hither. 17The woman answered and said, I have no husband. Jesus said unto her, Thou hast well said, I have no husband: 18For thou hast had five husbands; and he whom thou now hast is not thy husband: in that saidst thou truly. 19The woman saith unto him, Sir, I perceive that thou art a prophet. 20Our fathers worshipped in this mountain; and ye say, that in Jerusalem is the place where men ought to worship. 21Jesus saith unto her, Woman, believe me, the hour cometh, when ye shall neither in

patriarchs, were visited by God on this mountain, where later the first tabernacle was set up. But the Jews claim that God's only temple is in Jerusalem. Jesus said to her, Woman, remember this saying: The time will come when neither on this mountain nor at Jerusalem will be the place to worship. Worship the Father through me.

this mountain, nor yet at Jerusalem, worship the Father.

5You Samaritans do not understand God, although you claim to worship Him. Those who follow me know how to worship. Salvation does not belong to the Jews, but instead will come from a Messiah rejected by the Jews. The hour has arrived when the true worshipers are being taught how to worship the Father in spirit and in truth, for the Father wants mankind to know Him. The Father will share his Spirit with those who know him. His Spirit is truth and light. And they who worship him must worship in spirit and in truth.

22Ye worship ye know not what: we know what we worship: for salvation is of the Jews. 23But the hour cometh, and now is, when the true worshippers shall worship the Father in spirit and in truth: for the Father seeketh such to worship him. 24God is a Spirit: and they that worship him must worship him in spirit and in truth.

6The woman said to him, I know that a Messiah is prophesied to come, and when he comes he will restore all that has been lost since the time of Adam. Jesus responded, I am he: I am come to restore, to repair, to redeem, and I am come to gather.

25The woman saith unto him, I know that Messias cometh, which is called Christ: when he is come, he will tell us all things. 26Jesus saith unto her, I that speak unto thee am he.

7As he was talking with the woman his followers arrived and were surprised to see that he talked with this Samaritan woman, but no one questioned him about why he would teach and testify openly to her. The woman then abandoned her waterpot, and quickly went into the city to proclaim to them

27And upon this came his disciples, and marvelled that he talked with the woman: yet no man said, What seekest thou? or, Why talkest thou with her? 28The woman then left her waterpot, and went her way into the city, and saith to the men, 29Come, see a man, which told me all things that ever I did: is not this

about who was at the well. She testified to the men, Come see a man who spoke as a seer. I testify that he is the Messiah and ask you to come hear him for yourselves. Because she was influential, a great crowd went out to investigate the woman's testimony of him.

⁸In the meantime, his disciples brought food and told him that he ought to eat. But seeing the approaching crowd he said, I have food to eat you do not see. His companions asked one another, Has someone brought him food while we were gone? Jesus clarified, My strength comes by obeying the will of God who sent me to do his work. Doing that sustains me by his Holy Spirit, and protects me until I finish his work. Do not make the mistake of thinking there are four months still before the harvest. I want you to look at the approaching crowd. They are the field I have been sent to harvest; they are prepared and ready. For this reason I have come to this place. These people will accept a new dispensation and the truth. Anyone who helps me with the Father's work in harvesting souls will likewise save their own soul. The harvest saves both the planter and gatherer together. Remember the expression: One plants and another harvests. I send you to help with the harvest, but others have prepared this field. The prophets planted and these people have responded, and you join the labor of the prophets by now teaching these prepared people.

⁹Many of the Samaritans from Shechem accepted him because of

the Christ? ³⁰Then they went out of the city, and came unto him.

³¹In the mean while his disciples prayed him, saying, Master, eat. ³²But he said unto them, I have meat to eat that ye know not of. ³³Therefore said the disciples one to another, Hath any man brought him ought to eat? ³⁴Jesus saith unto them, My meat is to do the will of him that sent me, and to finish his work. ³⁵Say not ye, There are yet four months, and then cometh harvest? behold, I say unto you, Lift up your eyes, and look on the fields; for they are white already to harvest. ³⁶And he that reapeth receiveth wages, and gathereth fruit unto life eternal: that both he that soweth and he that reapeth may rejoice together. ³⁷And herein is that saying true, One soweth, and another reapeth. ³⁸I sent you to reap that whereon ye bestowed no labour: other men laboured, and ye are entered into their labours.

³⁹And many of the Samaritans of that city believed on him for the

the woman's testimony that he was a seer who prophesied to and about her. So when the Samaritan crowd came to hear him, they implored him to stay and teach them. And he stayed and taught for two days. Then many more believed because of what he taught. Then others said to the woman, Now we no longer depend on your testimony, but we have heard him teach us, and recognize that this is indeed the Messiah, the Savior who has come to rescue the world.

saying of the woman, which testified, He told me all that ever I did. 40So when the Samaritans were come unto him, they besought him that he would tarry with them: and he abode there two days. 41And many more believed because of his own word; 42And said unto the woman, Now we believe, not because of thy saying: for we have heard him ourselves, and know that this is indeed the Christ, the Saviour of the world.

10Jesus stayed two days with them teaching, worshipping, and having them baptized before he departed to return to Galilee. On the way home Jesus repeated the parable: A prophet is never honored in his home town. But when he arrived in Galilee, the Galileans were excited to see him because many of them had been at Jerusalem during the Passover and told the others about the miracles he did there.

43Now after two days he departed thence, and went into Galilee. 44For Jesus himself testified, that a prophet hath no honour in his own country. 45Then when he was come into Galilee, the Galilæans received him, having seen all the things that he did at Jerusalem at the feast: for they also went unto the feast.

11Jesus came again into Cana of Galilee, where he earlier had turned water into wine. There was a wealthy and respected man there whose son lay sick at Capernaum. When he heard that Jesus had come back from Judea to Galilee, he traveled to Galilee to beg him to come to his home at Capernaum and heal his son because the young man was near death. Jesus responded to him, Like other Jews who seek signs, you want me to physically travel to him and put on a display, but all that is necessary is for you to have faith in the power to heal. But the father begged, Sir, please come to my house so that my child does not die. Jesus

46So Jesus came again into Cana of Galilee, where he made the water wine. And there was a certain nobleman, whose son was sick at Capernaum. 47When he heard that Jesus was come out of Judæa into Galilee, he went unto him, and besought him that he would come down, and heal his son: for he was at the point of death. 48Then said Jesus unto him, Except ye see signs and wonders, ye will not believe. 49The nobleman saith unto him, Sir, come down ere my child die. 50Jesus saith unto him, Go thy way; thy son liveth. And the man believed the word that Jesus had spoken unto him, and he went his way. 51And as he was now going

replied, Go to your home without me, for your son will recover and live – I have faith this will happen even if you do not. And the man wanted to believe what Jesus said, and trusting it may be possible, he left to return home. While he traveled back to his house, his servants were hurrying to meet him, and said, Your son has recovered and is not going to die! The father asked them when his recovery began. The servants told him it was the day before, just after midday. The father knew this had been the very moment when Jesus spoke the words that his son would recover and live, and he realized Jesus was a messenger of God. And his entire family likewise shared this belief in Jesus. This was the second miracle Jesus performed when he returned from Judea to Galilee.

down, his servants met him, and told him, saying, Thy son liveth. ⁵²Then inquired he of them the hour when he began to amend. And they said unto him, Yesterday at the seventh hour the fever left him. ⁵³So the father knew that it was at the same hour, in the which Jesus said unto him, Thy son liveth: and himself believed, and his whole house. ⁵⁴This is again the second miracle that Jesus did, when he was come out of Judæa into Galilee.

¹²After this came the Feast of the Tabernacles, and Jesus made the pilgrimage to Jerusalem for the feast.

KJV Chapter 5

¹After this there was a feast of the Jews; and Jesus went up to Jerusalem.

RE Chapter 5

¹Now there is at Jerusalem, by the sheep market, a pool, named in Hebrew, Bethesda, where there were five porches. In these porches lay a great many disabled people who were blind, infirm, or lame, hoping for people to take pity on them. There was one man among them who had been lame for thirty-eight years. Jesus noticed him in particular, and knew that he had been afflicted for many years. He asked him, Do you want to be made whole? The man answered him, Sir, I would be grateful for any help. Jesus replied to him,

²Now there is at Jerusalem by the sheep market a pool, which is called in the Hebrew tongue Bethesda, having five porches. ³In these lay a great multitude of impotent folk, of blind, halt, withered, waiting for the moving of the water. ⁴For an angel went down at a certain season into the pool, and troubled the water: whosoever then first after the troubling of the water stepped in was made whole of whatsoever disease he had. ⁵And a certain man was there, which had an infirmity thirty and eight years. ⁶When Jesus saw him lie, and knew

Arise, take up your bedding and go forward. And as soon as Jesus spoke, the man was made whole, and picked up his bedding, and walked. But this happened on the Jewish Sabbath day. The Jews were therefore judgmental and confronted the man who was cured, accusing him, saying, It is the Sabbath day, it is not lawful for you to carry your bedding. He answered them, The man who restored me, said to me, Pick up your bedding and walk. Then the angry Jews said, Who told you, Pick up your bedding and walk? But the healed man was unable to identify who healed him because Jesus had walked away and mingled with the festival crowd. Shortly afterwards Jesus met him again in the temple, and said to him, Remember, you have been healed, but take care to follow God, do not be ungrateful or you will offend God. Those who were following and watching Jesus (for the Jews were on the watch for him when he entered Jerusalem) were told by the man that Jesus was his healer.

²Then these Jews were even more angry at Jesus, and conspired to kill him because he had violated their traditions about the Sabbath and they feared he did every thing to undermine their authority. But Jesus corrected them saying, My Father works on every day including the Sabbath, and I follow his example. This convinced the Jews to be even more determined to kill Jesus, because he had both violated their traditions about the Sabbath, and claimed God was his Father,

that he had been now a long time in that case, he saith unto him, Wilt thou be made whole? ⁷The impotent man answered him, Sir, I have no man, when the water is troubled, to put me into the pool: but while I am coming, another steppeth down before me. ⁸Jesus saith unto him, Rise, take up thy bed, and walk. ⁹And immediately the man was made whole, and took up his bed, and walked: and on the same day was the sabbath. ¹⁰The Jews therefore said unto him that was cured, It is the sabbath day: it is not lawful for thee to carry thy bed. ¹¹He answered them, He that made me whole, the same said unto me, Take up thy bed, and walk. ¹²Then asked they him, What man is that which said unto thee, Take up thy bed, and walk? ¹³And he that was healed wist not who it was: for Jesus had conveyed himself away, a multitude being in that place. ¹⁴Afterward Jesus findeth him in the temple, and said unto him, Behold, thou art made whole: sin no more, lest a worse thing come unto thee. ¹⁵The man departed, and told the Jews that it was Jesus, which had made him whole.

¹⁶And therefore did the Jews persecute Jesus, and sought to slay him, because he had done these things on the sabbath day. ¹⁷But Jesus answered them, My Father worketh hitherto, and I work. ¹⁸Therefore the Jews sought the more to kill him, because he not only had broken the sabbath, but said also that God was his Father, making himself equal with God.

which would make him equal with God.

3Then Jesus affirmed to them, In the name of Father Ahman I tell you, The Son does nothing of himself, but I am following the path that my Father walks. Every thing the Father has done, I am likewise to do. My Father loves His Son, and has revealed to me every thing he has done, and I have a work to do for me to finish the path of my Father. You may not believe me, but before the end you will be in awe of what I am sent to do. The Father has attained to the resurrection, and I am sent to do likewise. In this creation the Father has made me the Source and judge of the resurrection. You will be required to honor the Son, even as you honor the Father. Anyone who disrespects the Son also disrespects the Father who sent me.

4In the name of Father Ahman I testify to you, He who hearkens to my testimony, and trusts him who sent me, there is no end to his potential progression. His progress will not cease, for I demonstrate the pathway of Eternal lives.

5In the name of Father Ahman I testify to you, The time has arrived when even the spirits in Sheol will hear the voice of the Son of God. Those who hearken to my testimony shall also progress upward on the pathway. The Father has the power of endless life within himself, and he has empowered the Son to attain this identical state through progression on his pathway. I hold authority to judge mankind because I am Son Ahman.

19Then answered Jesus and said unto them, Verily, verily, I say unto you, The Son can do nothing of himself, but what he seeth the Father do: for what things soever he doeth, these also doeth the Son likewise. 20For the Father loveth the Son, and sheweth him all things that himself doeth: and he will shew him greater works than these, that ye may marvel. 21For as the Father raiseth up the dead, and quickeneth them; even so the Son quickeneth whom he will. 22For the Father judgeth no man, but hath committed all judgment unto the Son: 23That all men should honour the Son, even as they honour the Father. He that honoureth not the Son honoureth not the Father which hath sent him.

24Verily, verily, I say unto you, He that heareth my word, and believeth on him that sent me, hath everlasting life, and shall not come into condemnation; but is passed from death unto life.

25Verily, verily, I say unto you, The hour is coming, and now is, when the dead shall hear the voice of the Son of God: and they that hear shall live. 26For as the Father hath life in himself; so hath he given to the Son to have life in himself; 27And hath given him authority to execute judgment also, because he is the Son of man. 28Marvel not at this: for the hour is coming, in the which all that are in the graves shall hear his voice, 29And shall

Do not doubt this, for the time is fast approaching when the dead will also be taught by my voice. The dead will rise from the grave: first the faithful in the resurrection of the just, and then the faithless in the resurrection of the unjust. Every soul will be judged by Son Ahman. Whatever the Father tells me, I accept and teach, and my teachings are all just and true. I take nothing on myself apart from the Father's instruction. I do not pursue my own agenda, but the Father's agenda, for I act under his authority.

6Therefore I am a witness of the truth, and my witness is true. I am not a lone witness because my Father testifies to those who will listen. My works testify also. But you do not listen to my Father and you condemn my works. Therefore you reject the truth. You asked John, and he was also my witness of the truth. He did not receive his testimony from only a man, but directly from God, and you admit he is a prophet. Therefore you should accept his testimony.

7I am telling you these things to save you. John was a brilliant light sent from above, and you were willing to hear and acknowledge him for a short while. But there is even a greater reason than John's words to believe what I teach: As I complete the journey to finish the Father's path, those final steps will plainly testify of me.

8I testify of the truth. The Father testifies to those who will hear him. John testified of me. And the come forth; they that have done good, unto the resurrection of life; and they that have done evil, unto the resurrection of damnation. 30I can of mine own self do nothing: as I hear, I judge: and my judgment is just; because I seek not mine own will, but the will of the Father which hath sent me. 31If I bear witness of myself, my witness is not true.

32There is another that beareth witness of me; and I know that the witness which he witnesseth of me is true. 33Ye sent unto John, and he bare witness unto the truth.

34But I receive not testimony from man: but these things I say, that ye might be saved. 35He was a burning and a shining light: and ye were willing for a season to rejoice in his light. 36But I have greater witness than that of John: for the works which the Father hath given me to finish, the same works that I do, bear witness of me, that the Father hath sent me.

37And the Father himself, which hath sent me, hath borne witness of me. Ye have neither heard his

works I am performing testify. But you do not hearken to my message, nor hear the Father, nor accept John's message, and you ignore the evidence shown by my works. Therefore, you are deliberately blind and choose not to know my Father, because you have no faith in his truth and refuse to walk in his pathway.

9You should carefully review again the scriptures, for you suppose they can save your soul, but they were written to testify of me. Although I can save your soul, you refuse salvation because you are opposed to me. I am not looking for vain popularity, but offer salvation for your souls. I understand what is in your hearts, and because you do not love God you do not love truth.

10I have come to you because the Father sent me, and I glorify his name, but you reject that. If someone not sent by the Father comes to glorify himself by displaying his own wisdom, you respect him. How can you ever gain light and truth when you use one another as the final authority on truth, and ignore the light sent by the Most High God? I will not need to condemn you before the Father because Moses will do that. If you really believed Moses you would understand he prophesied and testified of me. Since you have perverted what Moses wrote, how can you hope to believe me?

11After these events, Jesus went over the Sea of Galilee, which was renamed the Sea of Tiberias. And a large group followed him because

voice at any time, nor seen his shape. 38And ye have not his word abiding in you: for whom he hath sent, him ye believe not.

39Search the scriptures; for in them ye think ye have eternal life: and they are they which testify of me. 40And ye will not come to me, that ye might have life. 41I receive not honour from men. 42But I know you, that ye have not the love of God in you.

43I am come in my Father's name, and ye receive me not: if another shall come in his own name, him ye will receive. 44How can ye believe, which receive honour one of another, and seek not the honour that cometh from God only? 45Do not think that I will accuse you to the Father: there is one that accuseth you, even Moses, in whom ye trust. 46For had ye believed Moses, ye would have believed me: for he wrote of me. 47 But if ye believe not his writings, how shall ye believe my words?

KJV Chapter 6

1After these things Jesus went over the sea of Galilee, which is the sea of Tiberias. 2And a great multitude followed him, because they saw his

they saw his miracles healing the injured and diseased. Jesus climbed up a mountain and there he taught his companions. And the feast was approaching. When Jesus noticed the throng approaching them, he asked Philip, Where can we buy bread to feed these approaching people? He asked Philip the question, but already planned what he was going to do. Philip answered him, Two hundred days' wages would not buy enough bread to even give each of them a little. Another companion, Andrew, Simon Peter's brother, said to him, There is a boy with us who has five barley loaves and two dried salted fish, which is obviously not enough to feed this crowd. Jesus said, Have the people sit down on the plentiful grass. About five thousand were seated. Jesus stood and looked up to Heaven, holding up the barley loaves. While blessing the loaves, he thanked his Father. Then he distributed food to his companions, and then passed through the multitude and gave to each of them their fill of barley bread and salted fish. When the multitude were filled, Jesus asked his disciples, Gather every thing that remains uneaten so nothing is wasted. When it had all been gathered, the remainder filled twelve baskets, many times what had started with, five barley loaves and two fish. Then some of the multitude fed by this miracle testified, This is surely fulfillment of the sign of the Messiah, God's King and Priest, who will restore Israel as a nation!

12When Jesus overheard that they wanted to force him to be their

miracles which he did on them that were diseased. 3And Jesus went up into a mountain, and there he sat with his disciples. 4And the passover, a feast of the Jews, was nigh. 5When Jesus then lifted up his eyes, and saw a great company come unto him, he saith unto Philip, Whence shall we buy bread, that these may eat? 6And this he said to prove him: for he himself knew what he would do. 7Philip answered him, Two hundred pennyworth of bread is not sufficient for them, that every one of them may take a little. 8One of his disciples, Andrew, Simon Peter's brother, saith unto him, 9There is a lad here, which hath five barley loaves, and two small fishes: but what are they among so many? 10And Jesus said, Make the men sit down. Now there was much grass in the place. So the men sat down, in number about five thousand. 11And Jesus took the loaves; and when he had given thanks, he distributed to the disciples, and the disciples to them that were set down; and likewise of the fishes as much as they would. 12When they were filled, he said unto his disciples, Gather up the fragments that remain, that nothing be lost. 13Therefore they gathered them together, and filled twelve baskets with the fragments of the five barley loaves, which remained over and above unto them that had eaten. 14Then those men, when they had seen the miracle that Jesus did, said, This is of a truth that prophet that should come into the world.

15When Jesus therefore perceived that they would come and take

king, he walked away, going back up the mountain alone. That evening when some of the throng were leaving, his companions departed in a boat across the sea toward Capernaum. It was after dark and Jesus was not with them in the boat. At the time the sea became turbulent because of a strong wind. So when they had rowed about four miles, they saw Jesus walking upon the sea and approaching their boat; they were afraid. But he said, I am that I am, do not be frightened. They recognized this was another promised sign to identify the Messiah, and understood the meaning of his greeting, and then they were at their destiny.

¹³The next day, when the throng left behind on the other side of the sea discussed leaving, they realized there was no other boat than the one his companions had used. They knew that Jesus had not been with them on the boat. They saw his companions leave without him. But he was now gone away also. And so, when other boats arrived from Tiberias near to where they were fed barley bread after the Messiah had blessed it, they took the available boats and went to Capernaum to try to locate Jesus. When they found him on the other side of the sea, they asked, Teacher, from what source did you come? Jesus replied, In the name of Father Ahman I tell you, You follow after me, not because you intend to obey what I teach, nor because you witnessed miracles and believe, but you are slaves to your bellies and want to be fed more barley bread. Do not be preoccu-

him by force, to make him a king, he departed again into a mountain himself alone. ¹⁶And when even was now come, his disciples went down unto the sea, ¹⁷And entered into a ship, and went over the sea toward Capernaum. And it was now dark, and Jesus was not come to them. ¹⁸And the sea arose by reason of a great wind that blew. ¹⁹So when they had rowed about five and twenty or thirty furlongs, they see Jesus walking on the sea, and drawing nigh unto the ship: and they were afraid. ²⁰But he saith unto them, It is I; be not afraid. ²¹Then they willingly received him into the ship: and immediately the ship was at the land whither they went.

²²The day following, when the people which stood on the other side of the sea saw that there was none other boat there, save that one whereinto his disciples were entered, and that Jesus went not with his disciples into the boat, but that his disciples were gone away alone; ²³(Howbeit there came other boats from Tiberias nigh unto the place where they did eat bread, after that the Lord had given thanks:) ²⁴ When the people therefore saw that Jesus was not there, neither his disciples, they also took shipping, and came to Capernaum, seeking for Jesus. ²⁵And when they had found him on the other side of the sea, they said unto him, Rabbi, when camest thou hither? ²⁶Jesus answered them and said, Verily, verily, I say unto you, Ye seek me, not because ye saw the miracles, but because ye did eat of the loaves, and were filled. ²⁷Labour not for the meat

pied with food for your bellies, but for food from God, that is, light and truth, leading to endless progression upward. I am Son Ahman and can give you sustaining light and truth, for God the Father has declared I am His Son.

14Then they asked him, What do we need to do to enter God's pathway of endless progress? Jesus answered and said, The pathway is before you in me, I teach and display what the Father wants you to witness and believe. They said in response, What sign will you give to us to confirm this pathway, so we can trust your message? What will you give to us? Our fathers were fed with manna in the desert for forty years. As the scripture states, He gave them bread from Heaven to eat. Feed us likewise.

15Then Jesus said to them, In the name of Father Ahman I tell you the truth, Moses was not the one who gave bread, it was my Father who did that. But now my Father is offering true life-giving bread from Heaven, which is light and truth. For the Bread of God is sent from the Heavenly Council to give light and truth to the world. They responded, Master, feed us with this bread forever.

16Jesus said bluntly to them, I am the bread that gives life; he that follows the path with me will never hunger for light; and any who believe on me shall never thirst for truth. Unfortunately, as I have already told you, even though you have seen me, you do not believe me. But my Father has provided some who will heed my words, and

which perisheth, but for that meat which endureth unto everlasting life, which the Son of man shall give unto you: for him hath God the Father sealed.

28Then said they unto him, What shall we do, that we might work the works of God? 29Jesus answered and said unto them, This is the work of God, that ye believe on him whom he hath sent. 30They said therefore unto him, What sign shewest thou then, that we may see, and believe thee? what dost thou work? 31Our fathers did eat manna in the desert; as it is written, He gave them bread from heaven to eat.

32Then Jesus said unto them, Verily, verily, I say unto you, Moses gave you not that bread from heaven; but my Father giveth you the true bread from heaven. 33For the bread of God is he which cometh down from heaven, and giveth life unto the world. 34Then said they unto him, Lord, evermore give us this bread.

35And Jesus said unto them, I am the bread of life: he that cometh to me shall never hunger; and he that believeth on me shall never thirst. 36But I said unto you, That ye also have seen me, and believe not. 37All that the Father giveth me shall come to me; and him that cometh to me I will in no wise cast out. 38-For I came down from heaven, not

those who follow me I will safely keep. I am descended from above as a Messenger sent to follow Father Ahman's plan. Father's plan is that by completing my ascent I will have the power to rescue creation, losing nothing. Moreover, those who are here on this journey with me will be added upon for evermore if they have faith in me. They will rise up to likewise generate endless lives, worlds without end.

¹⁷The Jews loudly objected to his claim of calling himself, I am, and equating himself with God, and because he claimed to be the bread which came down from Heaven. And they challenged his teaching, asking the people, Is not this Jesus, the son of Joseph, whose father and mother we know? How can he claim to descend from Heaven?

¹⁸Jesus responded to them, Do not dispute my teaching between yourselves. No man can come unto me except he follows the path of my Father, who has sent me as His messenger of salvation. And this is what my Father expects of you, that you heed his Son. For the Father testifies he sent me, and anyone who accepts the Father's testimony, and has the faith in him to heed his testimony, I will raise upward in the resurrection of the just. For it is written in the prophets, And these shall all be taught by God. Every person who has hearkened and has learned the will of the Father, accepts me as his messenger. None of you have seen the Father unless you first descended from God's presence, as I have come; and all who have seen the Father can testify of him. In the

to do mine own will, but the will of him that sent me. ³⁹And this is the Father's will which hath sent me, that of all which he hath given me I should lose nothing, but should raise it up again at the last day. ⁴⁰And this is the will of him that sent me, that every one which seeth the Son, and believeth on him, may have everlasting life: and I will raise him up at the last day.

⁴¹The Jews then murmured at him, because he said, I am the bread which came down from heaven. ⁴²And they said, Is not this Jesus, the son of Joseph, whose father and mother we know? how is it then that he saith, I came down from heaven?

⁴³Jesus therefore answered and said unto them, Murmur not among yourselves. ⁴⁴No man can come to me, except the Father which hath sent me draw him: and I will raise him up at the last day. ⁴⁵It is written in the prophets, And they shall be all taught of God. Every man therefore that hath heard, and hath learned of the Father, cometh unto me. ⁴⁶Not that any man hath seen the Father, save he which is of God, he hath seen the Father. ⁴⁷Verily, verily, I say unto you, He that believeth on me hath everlasting life. ⁴⁸I am that bread of life. ⁴⁹Your fathers did eat manna in the wilderness, and are dead. ⁵⁰This is the bread which cometh down from heaven, that a man may eat thereof, and not die. ⁵¹I am the living bread which came down from heaven: if any man eat

name of Father Ahman I declare to you, He that has faith on me has endless lives, worlds without end. I am that bread of life. This is the bread that descended from Heaven, that a man may eat of me and his life never end. Your fathers did eat manna in the wilderness and they perished. But I am the living bread sent from Heaven to rescue you. If any man takes into themselves this bread, he will gain light and truth and the power for endless life. The staff of life I provide is to sacrifice my flesh, which I will surrender to rescue the world.

19The Jews argued among themselves, demanding, How can this man give us his flesh to eat? Then Jesus said to them, In the name of Father Ahman I say unto you, Unless you eat the flesh of the Son of Man, and drink his blood, you will never have endless life in you. Those who eat my flesh, and drink my blood, will obtain endless life. I will raise him up in the resurrection of the just at the last day. Just as the Father provided this life for me, I will provide it for you if you have faith in me. For my flesh will fill you with light, and my blood will quench you with truth. If you receive these, I will fill you with light and truth and we will be brothers, sons of God. My sacrifice is the bread I descended from Heaven to provide, not like the manna eaten by your deceased ancestors who rejected greater light and truth in their day. The light and truth I offer leads to endless lives, worlds without end.

20The foregoing is what he taught in the Capernaum synagogue.

of this bread, he shall live for ever: and the bread that I will give is my flesh, which I will give for the life of the world.

52The Jews therefore strove among themselves, saying, How can this man give us his flesh to eat? 53Then Jesus said unto them, Verily, verily, I say unto you, Except ye eat the flesh of the Son of man, and drink his blood, ye have no life in you. 54Whoso eateth my flesh, and drinketh my blood, hath eternal life; and I will raise him up at the last day. 55For my flesh is meat indeed, and my blood is drink indeed. 56He that eateth my flesh, and drinketh my blood, dwelleth in me, and I in him. 57As the living Father hath sent me, and I live by the Father: so he that eateth me, even he shall live by me. 58This is that bread which came down from heaven: not as your fathers did eat manna, and are dead: he that eateth of this bread shall live for ever.

59These things said he in the synagogue, as he taught in Capernaum.

RE Chapter 6

¹Many of his followers, after they had heard him teach this in the synagogue, concluded, This is hard to accept; who can agree with it? When Jesus understood that even his close companions balked at it, he said to them, Are you offended by that? How are you going to have the faith to witness my ascent back to the Throne of the Father where I have come from? I have spoken of the Spirit of light and truth that enlightens. The flesh is nothing, and my message is about light and truth. My teachings are Spirit, and they are life. But there are some of you that do not understand because you do not believe. For Jesus knew from the beginning the ones who were faithless and foresaw who would betray him. And he said, Because of faithlessness I tell you that no faithless man can come with me. Only those who heed the will of my Father who sent me will have power to rise with me.

²At that time many followers left and ended their journey with him. Then Jesus asked the twelve, Are you also going to leave? To which Simon Peter answered, Lord, where else is there to go? You teach the words of Eternal life. All of us believe and are certain that you are the Messiah, the Holy One of the Most High God. Jesus told them, Have I not chosen you twelve, and even among you one follows the accuser? He spoke of Judas Iscariot, the son of Simon, for he was one of the twelve and would ultimately betray him.

⁶⁰Many therefore of his disciples, when they had heard this, said, This is an hard saying; who can hear it? ⁶¹When Jesus knew in himself that his disciples murmured at it, he said unto them, Doth this offend you? ⁶²What and if ye shall see the Son of man ascend up where he was before? ⁶³It is the spirit that quickeneth; the flesh profiteth nothing: the words that I speak unto you, they are spirit, and they are life. ⁶⁴But there are some of you that believe not. For Jesus knew from the beginning who they were that believed not, and who should betray him. ⁶⁵And he said, Therefore said I unto you, that no man can come unto me, except it were given unto him of my Father.

⁶⁶From that time many of his disciples went back, and walked no more with him. ⁶⁷Then said Jesus unto the twelve, Will ye also go away? ⁶⁸Then Simon Peter answered him, Lord, to whom shall we go? thou hast the words of eternal life. ⁶⁹And we believe and are sure that thou art that Christ, the Son of the living God. ⁷⁰Jesus answered them, Have not I chosen you twelve, and one of you is a devil? ⁷¹He spake of Judas Iscariot the son of Simon: for he it was that should betray him, being one of the twelve.

KJV Chapter 7

3After this upheaval among his followers, Jesus taught in Galilee, but he avoided Judea because the Jews viewed him as a threat to their authority and were conspiring to murder him. Now the Feast of Tabernacles was about to begin. His half-brothers expected him to attend the feast and mentioned to him, Let us leave here and go to Judea, that your followers there can witness your good works. Because nobody hides from the public and can expect to be noticed. If you are going to work wonders, you really should show yourself in Jerusalem. But these half-brothers did not really believe in him. Then Jesus responded, My time of sacrifice is not yet come, but you are always ready to criticize. The world does not hate you, but it does hate me because I proclaim against false religion and hypocrisy. You go to the feast without me. I am not going with you. The time has not arrived for my life to end. After that conversation, he went as if he were returning to Galilee.

4But after his half-brothers departed for Jerusalem, he turned and also headed for the feast, but traveled so as to be unnoticed. As was their practice, the Jews were on watch for him during the feast and were asking, Is he here? Have you seen him? Jesus was discussed by many people, debating whether he was a good man or a deceiver. But pilgrims avoided discussing him openly because they were afraid of the Jewish leaders who detested him.

1After these things Jesus walked in Galilee: for he would not walk in Jewry, because the Jews sought to kill him. 2Now the Jews' feast of tabernacles was at hand. 3His brethren therefore said unto him, Depart hence, and go into Judæa, that thy disciples also may see the works that thou doest. 4For there is no man that doeth any thing in secret, and he himself seeketh to be known openly. If thou do these things, shew thyself to the world. 5For neither did his brethren believe in him. 6Then Jesus said unto them, My time is not yet come: but your time is alway ready. 7The world cannot hate you; but me it hateth, because I testify of it, that the works thereof are evil. 8Go ye up unto this feast: I go not up yet unto this feast; for my time is not yet full come. 9When he had said these words unto them, he abode still in Galilee.

10But when his brethren were gone up, then went he also up unto the feast, not openly, but as it were in secret. 11Then the Jews sought him at the feast, and said, Where is he? 12And there was much murmuring among the people concerning him: for some said, He is a good man: others said, Nay; but he deceiveth the people. 13Howbeit no man spake openly of him for fear of the Jews.

5During the celebration of the feast, Jesus arrived and openly taught in the temple courtyard. Hearing what he taught, the Jewish leaders were surprised and posed the question, How can he understand these complex things so well when he never received learning from us? Jesus responded to their question, My doctrine does not come from me, but from God who sent me. Anyone who walks in God's path will understand his doctrine, because that path increases light and knowledge. I testify of that path. Follow it and you will know whether I am sent by God or I am not sent by God. Teachers who preach from their own understanding only gratify their pride, but a teacher of truth teaches only what God tells him, and that teacher provides a light worth heeding.

6Did not Moses give you commandments to follow, but you disobey them? How can you conspire to murder me when Moses' commandments forbid murder? The leaders defended themselves by responding, You are possessed by a lying devil. Who do you falsely claim is conspiring to murder you? Jesus replied to them, I did God's work and healed a man, and you were offended. Moses approved the practice of circumcision (it did not originate with Moses, but originated with the first Patriarchs at the beginning), but Moses continued the practice and you perform circumcision on the Sabbath. If you approve circumcising a man on the Sabbath day in order to obey the commandment of Moses, how can you disapprove of me

14Now about the midst of the feast Jesus went up into the temple, and taught. 15And the Jews marvelled, saying, How knoweth this man letters, having never learned? 16Jesus answered them, and said, My doctrine is not mine, but his that sent me. 17If any man will do his will, he shall know of the doctrine, whether it be of God, or whether I speak of myself. 18He that speaketh of himself seeketh his own glory: but he that seeketh his glory that sent him, the same is true, and no unrighteousness is in him.

19Did not Moses give you the law, and yet none of you keepeth the law? Why go ye about to kill me? 20The people answered and said, Thou hast a devil: who goeth about to kill thee? 21Jesus answered and said unto them, I have done one work, and ye all marvel. 22-Moses therefore gave unto you circumcision; (not because it is of Moses, but of the fathers;) and ye on the sabbath day circumcise a man. 23If a man on the sabbath day receive circumcision, that the law of Moses should not be broken; are ye angry at me, because I have made a man every whit whole on the sabbath day? 24Judge not according to the appearance, but judge righteous judgment.

healing a man on the Sabbath day, an act that makes him whole? Do not use your false traditions to decide if something is good, but use the light of God to decide if any action I take is approved by him.

⁷Then some of the residents of Jerusalem came upon this exchange and inquired, Is not this the man the leaders want to kill? How is he teaching so boldly while they fail to silence him? Are the leaders afraid that he really is the Messiah? And others said, No, he is from Galilee. The Messiah obviously will not come from there, but from Heaven. Jesus was in the temple as he taught, and he responded to these inquiries by saying, You are familiar with me, and you know I am from Galilee, but I have been sent by the Most High God and you refuse to acknowledge him. I know him. I am from him, and he has sent me. When they heard this, they wanted to kill him on the spot, but because the time for his sacrifice had not come they were held back. But there were those present who heard what he taught, and saw what he did, and believed, saying, When the Messiah comes, will he provide more evidence that he is sent by the Most High God than this man has provided?

⁸The Pharisees overheard the comments of these believers, and they directed their guards to detain Jesus. But when the guards came, Jesus said to them, I will only be here for a little while, and then I will return to him who sent me. You will then want me to be with you, but at that time you will

²⁵Then said some of them of Jerusalem, Is not this he, whom they seek to kill? ²⁶But, lo, he speaketh boldly, and they say nothing unto him. Do the rulers know indeed that this is the very Christ? ²⁷Howbeit we know this man whence he is: but when Christ cometh, no man knoweth whence he is. ²⁸Then cried Jesus in the temple as he taught, saying, Ye both know me, and ye know whence I am: and I am not come of myself, but he that sent me is true, whom ye know not. ²⁹But I know him: for I am from him, and he hath sent me. ³⁰Then they sought to take him: but no man laid hands on him, because his hour was not yet come. ³¹And many of the people believed on him, and said, When Christ cometh, will he do more miracles than these which this man hath done?

³²The Pharisees heard that the people murmured such things concerning him; and the Pharisees and the chief priests sent officers to take him. ³³Then said Jesus unto them, Yet a little while am I with you, and then I go unto him that sent me. ³⁴Ye shall seek me, and shall not find me: and where I am,

be disappointed. I will rise up to where you can never come. Then the leaders mocked his response, How can he rise up to a place we cannot go? Will he travel among the scattered Israelites to trouble them? Or try to make gentile converts? What foolishness he utters by claiming he can rise up where we can never come. We would not want to be with him. If he leaves us, why would we ever try to again be with him?

9 During the last day of the feast, Jesus proclaimed to the throng, If any man thirsts, let him come to me and drink. Anyone who believes on me, as the scripture promises, out of his belly shall flow rivers of living water (he was speaking of the Holy Spirit, which believers were promised. Following Jesus' resurrection, Divine Wisdom was promised to fill believers).

10This produced controversy with some saying, He is certainly the prophet who Moses said we must heed or be cut off. Others said, He is the Messiah. But others said, He is not true because prophecy never stated the Messiah will come from Galilee. Does not the prophecy predict the Messiah will be a descendant of David and be from Bethlehem? The people were divided because of him. And some of them wanted to arrest him, but no one laid hands on him.

11At a meeting of the Sanhedrin the guards were asked, Why have you not detained him and brought him to us? The officers answered, We have never heard any man speak

thither ye cannot come. 35Then said the Jews among themselves, Whither will he go, that we shall not find him? will he go unto the dispersed among the Gentiles, and teach the Gentiles? 36What manner of saying is this that he said, Ye shall seek me, and shall not find me: and where I am, thither ye cannot come?

37In the last day, that great day of the feast, Jesus stood and cried, saying, If any man thirst, let him come unto me, and drink. 38He that believeth on me, as the scripture hath said, out of his belly shall flow rivers of living water. 39(But this spake he of the Spirit, which they that believe on him should receive: for the Holy Ghost was not yet given; because that Jesus was not yet glorified.)

40Many of the people therefore, when they heard this saying, said, Of a truth this is the Prophet. 41Others said, This is the Christ. But some said, Shall Christ come out of Galilee? 42Hath not the scripture said, That Christ cometh of the seed of David, and out of the town of Bethlehem, where David was? 43So there was a division among the people because of him. 44And some of them would have taken him; but no man laid hands on him.

45Then came the officers to the chief priests and Pharisees; and they said unto them, Why have ye not brought him? 46The officers answered, Never man spake like

like he does. Then members of the Sanhedrin said, Are you also deceived? Have any of us who are members of the Sanhedrin believed on him? Only the ignorant public, who do not keep the law as we do, are misled to believe him. Nicodemus, who had earlier come to speak with Jesus, asked, Does our law condemn a man before he can defend himself or respond to the accusations against him? They asked him, Are you also from Galilee? Search and look. There is no prophet foretold to come from Galilee. Their debate ended with that and everyone went home.

12Jesus spent that night on the Mount of Olives. Early in the morning he returned to the temple. A crowd gathered to hear him teach, and he sat down and taught them.

this man. 47Then answered them the Pharisees, Are ye also deceived? 48Have any of the rulers or of the Pharisees believed on him? 49But this people who knoweth not the law are cursed. 50Nicodemus saith unto them, (he that came to Jesus by night, being one of them,) 51Doth our law judge any man, before it hear him, and know what he doeth? 52They answered and said unto him, Art thou also of Galilee? Search, and look: for out of Galilee ariseth no prophet. 53And every man went unto his own house.

KJV Chapter 8

1Jesus went unto the mount of Olives. 2And early in the morning he came again into the temple, and all the people came unto him; and he sat down, and taught them.

3And the scribes and Pharisees brought unto him a woman taken in adultery; and when they had set her in the midst, 4They say unto him, Master, this woman was taken in adultery, in the very act. 5Now Moses in the law commanded us, that such should be stoned: but what sayest thou? 6This they said, tempting him, that they might have to accuse him. But Jesus stooped down, and with his finger wrote on the ground, as though he heard them not. 7So when they continued asking him, he lifted up himself, and said unto them, He that is without sin among you, let him first cast a stone at her. 8And again he stooped down, and wrote on the ground. 9And they which heard it, being convicted by their own conscience, went out one by one, beginning at the eldest, even unto the last: and Jesus was left alone, and the woman standing in the midst. [10]When Jesus had lifted up himself, and saw none but the woman, he said unto her, Woman, where are those thine accusers? hath no man condemned thee? [11]She said, No man, Lord. And Jesus said unto her, Neither do I condemn thee: go, and sin no more.

Jesus again testified to them, I am the light of the world; he that follows me will not walk in darkness, but shall be guided by the light of life.

[12]Then spake Jesus again unto them, saying, I am the light of the world: he that followeth me shall not walk in darkness, but shall have the light of life.

[13]The Pharisees challenged him by interrupting, You testify of yourself. The law requires two witnesses and therefore your testimony cannot be true. Jesus replied to them, Even though I testify of myself, my testimony is nevertheless true and binding, for I know where I came from and where I am going, but you do not understand where I came from nor where I am going. You debate about geography rather than understanding that I come from God who sent me. For the present I withhold from condemning you leaders. But if I were to condemn you, I would be right to do so.

[13]The Pharisees therefore said unto him, Thou bearest record of thyself; thy record is not true. [14]Jesus answered and said unto them, Though I bear record of myself, yet my record is true: for I know whence I came, and whither I go; but ye cannot tell whence I come, and whither I go. [15]Ye judge after the flesh; I judge no man. [16]And yet if I judge, my judgment is true: for I am not alone, but I and the Father that sent me.

[14]As for your claim that I am my only witness, I am not alone, but the Father is also my witness. It is true the law you claim to follow requires two witnesses. I am one, and the Father who sent me also testifies as a witness of me. They asked him, Where is your Father? Jesus answered, You do not know either me or my Father because if

[17]It is also written in your law, that the testimony of two men is true. [18]I am one that bear witness of myself, and the Father that sent me beareth witness of me. [19]Then said they unto him, Where is thy Father? Jesus answered, Ye neither know me, nor my Father: if ye had known me, ye should have known my Father also. [20]These words

you knew who I am you would understand who the Father is also. He declared this while in the temple treasury as he taught in the temple courtyard. The Sanhedrin failed to detain him because the time for his sacrifice had not yet arrived.

15Then Jesus repeated to them, I will continue onward following the path of my Father, and you will not accompany me, but will instead die under the burden of your sins. Therefore you cannot go where I will be. Then the Sanhedrin scornfully asked, Does he plan to kill himself? Is that why he said, The path he will take we will not join? And Jesus responded to them, You are from a lower estate. I am from the Heavens. You are stuck in this world, and I am not of this world. Because of this I said to you that you will die burdened with sins. If you do not believe that I am sent by the Most High God, bringing light and life with me, you will die burdened with sins. They said to him, So tell us who you claim to be. And Jesus answered them, I am the same as I told you from the beginning.

16I have many things to teach that will be used to judge you; and the one who sent me is the Source of all truth. I am teaching what he has sent me to teach and he provided my message. They did not understand that he was speaking the words of Father Ahman. Then Jesus added, When you have lifted up the Son of Man, then you will realize that I am Son Ahman, and that I have done nothing on my own; but as my Father has taught me, I repeat his words. He sent me

spake Jesus in the treasury, as he taught in the temple: and no man laid hands on him; for his hour was not yet come.

21Then said Jesus again unto them, I go my way, and ye shall seek me, and shall die in your sins: whither I go, ye cannot come. 22Then said the Jews, Will he kill himself? because he saith, Whither I go, ye cannot come. 23And he said unto them, Ye are from beneath; I am from above: ye are of this world; I am not of this world. 24I said therefore unto you, that ye shall die in your sins: for if ye believe not that I am he, ye shall die in your sins. 25Then said they unto him, Who art thou? And Jesus saith unto them, Even the same that I said unto you from the beginning.

26I have many things to say and to judge of you: but he that sent me is true; and I speak to the world those things which I have heard of him. 27They understood not that he spake to them of the Father. 28Then said Jesus unto them, When ye have lifted up the Son of man, then shall ye know that I am he, and that I do nothing of myself; but as my Father hath taught me, I speak these things. 29And he that sent me is with me: the Father

and accompanies me here; the Father has never abandoned my side. I always do the things that please him.

17When he spoke these words, many believed on him.

18Then Jesus addressed those Jews who believed on him, Only if you continue to follow my teachings will you be my students indeed, because you will know the truth, and the truth will make you free. The leaders interrupted to claim, We are Abraham's descendants, and have never been slaves to any man. Why do you say we will become free? Jesus answered them, In the name of Father Ahman I say unto you, Whoever misses the mark is the slave of errors. And such a slave will not be allowed to be within Abraham's house in the resurrection, but the Son will remain part of God's Family forever.

19If the Son sets you free from sin, you are free indeed. I know that you are Abraham's descendants, but you conspire to kill me because my teachings have no place within you. I teach you what the Father has shown to me while I was in his presence, and you follow the teaching of your father. They answered and said to him, Abraham is our father. Jesus replied to them, If you were really Abraham's children, you would do the works of Abraham. But instead you plan to kill me. And why do you plan to kill me: I am a man that has only told you the truth that I have heard from the Most High God; Abraham would never do such a thing. You follow the example of your real

hath not left me alone; for I do always those things that please him.

30As he spake these words, many believed on him.

31Then said Jesus to those Jews which believed on him, If ye continue in my word, then are ye my disciples indeed; 32And ye shall know the truth, and the truth shall make you free. 33They answered him, We be Abraham's seed, and were never in bondage to any man: how sayest thou, Ye shall be made free? 34Jesus answered them, Verily, verily, I say unto you, Whosoever committeth sin is the servant of sin. 35And the servant abideth not in the house for ever: but the Son abideth ever.

36If the Son therefore shall make you free, ye shall be free indeed. 37I know that ye are Abraham's seed; but ye seek to kill me, because my word hath no place in you. 38I speak that which I have seen with my Father: and ye do that which ye have seen with your father. 39They answered and said unto him, Abraham is our father. Jesus saith unto them, If ye were Abraham's children, ye would do the works of Abraham. 40But now ye seek to kill me, a man that hath told you the truth, which I have heard of God: this did not Abraham. 41Ye do the deeds of your father. Then said they to him, We be not born of fornication; we have one Father, even God. 42Jesus said unto them, If God

father. Then they said to him, You are the product of extramarital fornication involving an unknown number of men, and we are not. We have one Father, even God. Jesus said to them, If God were your Father, you would love me, for I am sent by and represent God. I am not speaking my own words or pursuing my own agenda, but the Father's words and agenda. Why do you fail to comprehend my words? Your refusal to hearken and submit to my teachings makes you deaf indeed. Your father is the accuser, and you share the envy and rebellion of your father. He was a rebellious destroyer from the beginning, and fought against the truth, because he prefers lies. When he spreads a lie, he advances his agenda. He is the source of deceit in this fallen world. And because I am the Source of truth, you are unable to believe me. Which of you can truthfully show that I have missed the mark? And if I teach the truth, why do you refuse to believe me? Everyone who follows the Most High God hearkens to God's words. Because you do not follow the Most High God, you cannot hear him.

20Then the leaders retorted, When we refer to you as a Samaritan possessed by a devil we have accurately described you. Jesus answered, I have no devil guiding me; I obey my Father, and you dishonor both him and me. I do not pursue acclaim or honor. You are the ones that seek acclaim and wrongly judge me. In the name of Father Ahman I say to you, If anyone stands watch awaiting direction from me, he shall not be overtaken

were your Father, ye would love me: for I proceeded forth and came from God; neither came I of myself, but he sent me. 43Why do ye not understand my speech? even because ye cannot hear my word. 44Ye are of your father the devil, and the lusts of your father ye will do. He was a murderer from the beginning, and abode not in the truth, because there is no truth in him. When he speaketh a lie, he speaketh of his own: for he is a liar, and the father of it. 45And because I tell you the truth, ye believe me not. 46Which of you convinceth me of sin? And if I say the truth, why do ye not believe me? 47 He that is of God heareth God's words: ye therefore hear them not, because ye are not of God.

48Then answered the Jews, and said unto him, Say we not well that thou art a Samaritan, and hast a devil? 49Jesus answered, I have not a devil; but I honour my Father, and ye do dishonour me. 50And I seek not mine own glory: there is one that seeketh and judgeth. 51Verily, verily, I say unto you, If a man keep my saying, he shall never see death. 52Then said the Jews unto him, Now we know that thou hast a devil. Abraham is dead, and

even by death, throughout eons. Then the leaders of the Jews said to him, Now we know that you are possessed by a devil. Abraham is dead, along with the prophets who were God's chosen. Yet you claim, If a man awaits direction from you, he shall not be overtaken by death through the eons. Do you claim you are greater than our father Abraham who was overtaken by death, greater than the prophets who are dead? Is there no limit to your vainglory? Jesus replied, If I honor myself, my honor is nothing. It is my Father who honors me, the one who you falsely claim is your God. Unlike me, you do not know him. If I were to say, I do not know him, I would be as much of a liar as you are when you falsely claim him as your God. I not only know him, but I watch for his words like a sentinel always awaiting his direction. Your father Abraham rejoiced to see my day, and he saw it and was glad. Then the leaders of the Jews mocked him saying, You are not yet fifty years old, and yet you claim to have seen Abraham? Jesus said unto them, In the name of Father Ahman I say unto you, Before Abraham was, he knew me as I am. Then they picked up stones to throw at him because they regarded his statement as blasphemy. But Jesus hid from their view and safely departed from the temple, bypassing the crowd undetected.

the prophets; and thou sayest, If a man keep my saying, he shall never taste of death. 53Art thou greater than our father Abraham, which is dead? and the prophets are dead: whom makest thou thyself? 54Jesus answered, If I honour myself, my honour is nothing: it is my Father that honoureth me; of whom ye say, that he is your God: 55Yet ye have not known him; but I know him: and if I should say, I know him not, I shall be a liar like unto you: but I know him, and keep his saying. 56Your father Abraham rejoiced to see my day: and he saw it, and was glad. 57Then said the Jews unto him, Thou art not yet fifty years old, and hast thou seen Abraham? 58Jesus said unto them, Verily, verily, I say unto you, Before Abraham was, I am. 59Then took they up stones to cast at him: but Jesus hid himself, and went out of the temple, going through the midst of them, and so passed by.

RE Chapter 7

¹And as Jesus departed Jerusalem, he saw a man who had been born blind. His followers inquired, Master, who sinned, this man or his parents, to cause him to be born blind? Jesus answered, Neither this man nor his parents caused this affliction, but his infirmity allows the mercy of God to be displayed by making him whole. I must perform the works of him that sent me while I am with you. The time is coming when I will have finished my work here, then I will return to the Father. As long as I am in the world, I am the giver of light in the world. When he said this he spat on the ground and made clay of the spittle. Then he anointed the eyes of the blind man with the clay and said to him, Go, wash in the pool of Siloam (which is by interpretation, Sent). The blind man left for the pool and washed, and he began to see.

²The people who knew him and were aware of his blindness asked, Is not this the blind beggar? Some said, Yes it is him; others said, No he only resembles him, but the man said, I am he. Those who knew him asked, How did you obtain your sight? He answered and said, A man named Jesus made clay and anointed my eyes and said to me, Go to the pool of the Sent One and wash. I went and washed and I received sight. Then they asked him, Where is that man? He said, I do not know.

³And they brought the formerly blind man to the Sanhedrin be-

KJV Chapter 9

¹And as Jesus passed by, he saw a man which was blind from his birth. ²And his disciples asked him, saying, Master, who did sin, this man, or his parents, that he was born blind? ³Jesus answered, Neither hath this man sinned, nor his parents: but that the works of God should be made manifest in him. ⁴I must work the works of him that sent me, while it is day: the night cometh, when no man can work. ⁵As long as I am in the world, I am the light of the world. ⁶When he had thus spoken, he spat on the ground, and made clay of the spittle, and he anointed the eyes of the blind man with the clay, ⁷And said unto him, Go, wash in the pool of Siloam, (which is by interpretation, Sent.) He went his way therefore, and washed, and came seeing.

⁸The neighbours therefore, and they which before had seen him that he was blind, said, Is not this he that sat and begged? ⁹Some said, This is he: others said, He is like him: but he said, I am he. ¹⁰Therefore said they unto him, How were thine eyes opened? ¹¹He answered and said, A man that is called Jesus made clay, and anointed mine eyes, and said unto me, Go to the pool of Siloam, and wash: and I went and washed, and I received sight. ¹²Then said they unto him, Where is he? He said, I know not.

¹³They brought to the Pharisees him that aforetime was blind.

cause once again Jesus healed the blind man on the Sabbath day. The leaders again asked the man the same question: How were you healed of blindness? He answered them, There was a man who put clay on my eyes, and I washed and was no longer blind.

4Some of the Sanhedrin declared, That man cannot be of God because he breaks the commandment to never work on the Sabbath. But others said, How can a sinful man do such miracles? And there was a disagreement among them. They then asked the blind man again, Do you think the man who healed you was a sinner? He responded, He is a prophet.

5But the leaders avoided settling the argument by deciding everything was a lie: Therefore the man had never been blind and did not have his sight restored. Then the parents of the man born blind were asked, Is this your son who is claimed to have been born blind? How then does he now see? His parents answered, We know that this is our son and that he was born blind. But how he now has vision we do not know, nor do we know who cured his blindness. He is old enough to speak for himself so ask him, he should speak for himself. The parents were afraid of the leaders because the Sanhedrin had threatened to excommunicate anyone who claimed Jesus was the Messiah. This is why they said, He is old enough to speak for himself so ask him.

6Then they threatened the man that had been blind telling him,

14And it was the sabbath day when Jesus made the clay, and opened his eyes. 15Then again the Pharisees also asked him how he had received his sight. He said unto them, He put clay upon mine eyes, and I washed, and do see.

16Therefore said some of the Pharisees, This man is not of God, because he keepeth not the sabbath day. Others said, How can a man that is a sinner do such miracles? And there was a division among them. 17They say unto the blind man again, What sayest thou of him, that he hath opened thine eyes? He said, He is a prophet.

18But the Jews did not believe concerning him, that he had been blind, and received his sight, until they called the parents of him that had received his sight. 19And they asked them, saying, Is this your son, who ye say was born blind? how then doth he now see? 20His parents answered them and said, We know that this is our son, and that he was born blind: 21But by what means he now seeth, we know not; or who hath opened his eyes, we know not: he is of age; ask him: he shall speak for himself. 22These words spake his parents, because they feared the Jews: for the Jews had agreed already, that if any man did confess that he was Christ, he should be put out of the synagogue. 23Therefore said his parents, He is of age; ask him.

24Then again called they the man that was blind, and said unto him,

Give God the praise; we know that this man is a sinner. He responded, Whether he is a sinner or not, I would not know. All I know is that I was blind, but now I can see. Then they asked him again, What did he do to heal you? How was he able to cause you to see? He answered them, I have told you already, and you do not believe. Will you believe if I repeat it and tell you again? And would that cause you to become one of his followers? Then they reviled him and said, You are his follower, but we follow Moses. We know that God spoke to Moses. As for this man we do not know where he comes from. The man answered and said to them, Why this is indeed a marvelous thing, that you do not know anything about the man, yet he has cured my blindness. But you teach that God does not listen to sinners, but if a man is obedient to God then God will answer his prayers. Since the world began, no man has restored eyesight to anyone born blind other than a prophet of God. If this man was not sent by God he could not have performed a miracle. The leaders reviled him by declaring, You were altogether born in sins, and are you attempting to teach us, who are not sinful? And they cast him out.

7Jesus heard he had been cast out, and when he found him, he said to him, Do you believe on the Son of God? He replied, Who is he, Lord, that I might believe on him? And Jesus said to him, You have both seen him and spoken with him, and I am he. And the man said, Lord, I believe. And he knelt down and worshipped him.

Give God the praise: we know that this man is a sinner. 25He answered and said, Whether he be a sinner or no, I know not: one thing I know, that, whereas I was blind, now I see. 26Then said they to him again, What did he to thee? how opened he thine eyes? 27He answered them, I have told you already, and ye did not hear: wherefore would ye hear it again? will ye also be his disciples? 28Then they reviled him, and said, Thou art his disciple; but we are Moses' disciples. 29We know that God spake unto Moses: as for this fellow, we know not from whence he is. 30The man answered and said unto them, Why herein is a marvellous thing, that ye know not from whence he is, and yet he hath opened mine eyes. 31Now we know that God heareth not sinners: but if any man be a worshipper of God, and doeth his will, him he heareth. 32Since the world began was it not heard that any man opened the eyes of one that was born blind. 33If this man were not of God, he could do nothing. 34They answered and said unto him, Thou wast altogether born in sins, and dost thou teach us? And they cast him out.

35Jesus heard that they had cast him out; and when he had found him, he said unto him, Dost thou believe on the Son of God? 36He answered and said, Who is he, Lord, that I might believe on him 37And Jesus said unto him, Thou hast both seen him, and it is he that talketh with thee. 38And he said, Lord, I believe. And he worshipped him.

8Jesus said, I am here in the world to prove who is righteous and who is not. Those who have been blinded by falsehoods I can teach them to see, and for those claiming they see clearly, I will leave them in their blindness. And some of the leaders who were nearby overheard him say this, and asked him, Are we blind also? Jesus said to them, If you were blind, you would not have sinned. But because you claim, We see, therefore your sins remain.

9In the name of Father Ahman I tell you, If you do not enter by the doorway into the protective sheepfold, but climb in any other way, then you are only a thief and a robber. But when you enter at the door and the shepherd lets you enter, then you belong. The shepherd guards the entry, and his sheep respond to his voice. He calls his sheep by name and leads them up. He leads his sheep by his example and asks them to follow in his path, and they follow because they trust his words. His sheep will not follow another, but will flee from a stranger. They do not recognize the stranger's voice. Jesus told this parable to them, but they could not understand what he meant by the parable.

10Then Jesus spoke to them again, In the name of Father Ahman I tell you, I am the door of the sheepfold. Every teacher now or before who has not testified of me are only thieves and robbers trying to take my sheep away, but my sheep

39And Jesus said, For judgment I am come into this world, that they which see not might see; and that they which see might be made blind. 40And some of the Pharisees which were with him heard these words, and said unto him, Are we blind also? 41Jesus said unto them, If ye were blind, ye should have no sin: but now ye say, We see; therefore your sin remaineth.

KJV Chapter 10

1Verily, verily, I say unto you, He that entereth not by the door into the sheepfold, but climbeth up some other way, the same is a thief and a robber. 2But he that entereth in by the door is the shepherd of the sheep. 3To him the porter openeth; and the sheep hear his voice: and he calleth his own sheep by name, and leadeth them out. 4And when he putteth forth his own sheep, he goeth before them, and the sheep follow him: for they know his voice. 5And a stranger will they not follow, but will flee from him: for they know not the voice of strangers. 6This parable spake Jesus unto them: but they understood not what things they were which he spake unto them.

7Then said Jesus unto them again, Verily, verily, I say unto you, I am the door of the sheep. 8All that ever came before me are thieves and robbers: but the sheep did not hear them. 9I am the door: by me if any man enter in, he shall be saved,

have refused to heed them. I am the door. Any man who enters the sheepfold through me shall be saved and shall continue to progress and be supported. The thief only intends to steal, slay, and consume the sheep. I have come to preserve the lives of my sheep so that they might have abundant life.

11I am the good shepherd, and a good shepherd will sacrifice his own life for the lives of his sheep. The true shepherd does not profit from the sheep, regarding them only as property, and cares nothing for the lives of the sheep. The false shepherd runs away when he sees a wolf approaching, letting the wolf destroy and scatter the sheep. I am the good shepherd and know my sheep, and they know me. But he who profits from the sheep flees, because he is only self-interested and cares nothing about the sheep. Just as the Father laid down his life for me, he trusts me with the lives of the sheep. I will sacrifice my life for the sheep.

12I have other sheep that are not part of this fold. I will visit them and they will also hear my voice, and I will make all my sheep into one fold, following one shepherd. My Father loves and trusts me with the flock because I will sacrifice my life for them, and then take it up again to provide life for the flock. No one will take my life, but instead I will offer it as a willing sacrifice. I have made the choice to lay it down, and I possess the power to take it up again. I received this commandment from my Father.

and shall go in and out, and find pasture. 10The thief cometh not, but for to steal, and to kill, and to destroy: I am come that they might have life, and that they might have it more abundantly.

11 I am the good shepherd: the good shepherd giveth his life for the sheep. 12But he that is an hireling, and not the shepherd, whose own the sheep are not, seeth the wolf coming, and leaveth the sheep, and fleeth: and the wolf catcheth them, and scattereth the sheep. 13The hireling fleeth, because he is an hireling, and careth not for the sheep. 14I am the good shepherd, and know my sheep, and am known of mine. 15As the Father knoweth me, even so know I the Father: and I lay down my life for the sheep.

16And other sheep I have, which are not of this fold: them also I must bring, and they shall hear my voice; and there shall be one fold, and one shepherd. 17Therefore doth my Father love me, because I lay down my life, that I might take it again. 18No man taketh it from me, but I lay it down of myself. I have power to lay it down, and I have power to take it again. This commandment have I received of my Father.

¹³There was a debate among the leaders of the Jews because of Jesus' teachings. Most of them concluded that He has a devil in him, and it makes him a madman. They asked, Why listen to him? Others said, What he teaches are not the words of a devil or madman. Besides, would a devil restore sight to the blind?

¹⁴Another confrontation happened at Jerusalem during the wintertime Feast of the Dedication. Jesus walked in the temple on Solomon's porch. The Jewish leaders came and surrounded him and said, How long do you intend to leave us guessing? If you are the Messiah, tell us plainly. Jesus answered them, I have already told you, and you did not believe. Consider the deeds I have accomplished in my Father Ahman's name, they identify me. But you will not believe even what you have seen me do, because you are not part of the flock given to me by the Father, as I have also told you before. My sheep respond to my voice, and I know them, and they follow me; and I cause them to have life. They shall never die throughout the eons, neither can any adversary remove them out of my hand. My Father, who gave them to me, is greater than all, and no adversary is able to take them out of my Father's hand. My Father and I are one.

¹⁵Then the leaders of the Jews picked up stones again to execute him. Jesus rebuked them saying, Many good works have I showed you from my Father. For which of those acts are you going to stone

¹⁹There was a division therefore again among the Jews for these sayings. ²⁰And many of them said, He hath a devil, and is mad; why hear ye him? ²¹Others said, These are not the words of him that hath a devil. Can a devil open the eyes of the blind?

²²And it was at Jerusalem the feast of the dedication, and it was winter. ²³And Jesus walked in the temple in Solomon's porch. ²⁴Then came the Jews round about him, and said unto him, How long dost thou make us to doubt? If thou be the Christ, tell us plainly. ²⁵Jesus answered them, I told you, and ye believed not: the works that I do in my Father's name, they bear witness of me.

²⁶But ye believe not, because ye are not of my sheep, as I said unto you. ²⁷My sheep hear my voice, and I know them, and they follow me: ²⁸And I give unto them eternal life; and they shall never perish, neither shall any man pluck them out of my hand. ²⁹My Father, which gave them me, is greater than all; and no man is able to pluck them out of my Father's hand. ³⁰I and my Father are one.

³¹Then the Jews took up stones again to stone him. ³²Jesus answered them, Many good works have I shewed you from my Father; for which of those works do ye stone me? ³³The Jews answered

me? The Jews answered him, We are not offended by good acts, but by your blasphemy which the law condemns with stoning. It is blasphemy for you, a man, to claim to be God. Jesus responded, Is it not written in the scriptures, I said you are gods? If God referred to those he spoke with as gods, and the scriptures are reliably true, how can you claim that I, who the Father sent as a witness of truth, commit blasphemy when I refer to myself as God's son? Judge me by what I do, and if I fail to do what God expects, then you do not need to believe me. But if I do what God tells me to do, even if you reject my words, consider my actions. They will convince you that God is within me, and I am within the Father. Whereupon they attempted again to detain him, but he escaped their hand and went away again beyond Jordan to the place where John first baptized. And he remained there. Many visited with him there. The visitors heard him teach and remarked, John did no miracle, but every thing that John said about this man is true. Many were converted during the time he stayed there.

him, saying, For a good work we stone thee not; but for blasphemy; and because that thou, being a man, makest thyself God. 34Jesus answered them, Is it not written in your law, I said, Ye are gods? 35If he called them gods, unto whom the word of God came, and the scripture cannot be broken; 36Say ye of him, whom the Father hath sanctified, and sent into the world, Thou blasphemest; because I said, I am the Son of God? 37If I do not the works of my Father, believe me not. 38But if I do, though ye believe not me, believe the works: that ye may know, and believe, that the Father is in me, and I in him. 39Therefore they sought again to take him: but he escaped out of their hand, 40And went away again beyond Jordan into the place where John at first baptized; and there he abode. 41And many resorted unto him, and said, John did no miracle: but all things that John spake of this man were true. 42And many believed on him there.

RE Chapter 8

1Now a man named Lazarus, living in Bethany, who was the brother of Mary and Martha, was sick. It was in their house that Mary, the Elect Lady, anointed Jesus with sacred oil and cut his hair. Mary and Martha lived together in the Bethany house, and Lazarus was in their house while ill. The sisters sent a message to Jesus saying, Lord, have pity, our brother you

KJV Chapter 11

1Now a certain man was sick, named Lazarus, of Bethany, the town of Mary and her sister Martha. 2(It was that Mary which anointed the Lord with ointment, and wiped his feet with her hair, whose brother Lazarus was sick.) 3Therefore his sisters sent unto him, saying, Lord, behold, he whom thou lovest is sick. 4When Jesus heard that, he said, This

love is gravely ill. And when Jesus heard of the sickness, he said, This sickness will not cause his death, but it will show the glory of God, and will make it clear that the Son of God is glorified by the Father.

sickness is not unto death, but for the glory of God, that the Son of God might be glorified thereby.

2Now Jesus loved the entire family, Martha, her sister, and Lazarus. Jesus waited two days after he heard Lazarus was sick, remaining where he was when first informed of the illness. After that delay he said to his followers, Now let us go to Judea again. But his disciples reminded him, Master, the Jews recently attempted to stone you; and you want to return there again? Jesus answered, Are there only twelve hours of light each day? During the daylight a man can see to walk and does not stumble and fall because the daylight informs him. But at night, without the light, a man stumbles because of the darkness surrounding him. He said these things, and he said also to them, Our friend Lazarus is now sleeping, but I will go to awaken him from his sleep. Then his disciples said, Lord, if he is sleeping he will be fine. However Jesus meant that he had died, but they thought he meant resting in sleep. Then Jesus said bluntly, Lazarus is dead. And I am glad for your sakes that I was not there, so that now you will believe; nevertheless let us go to him. Thomas, who is called Didymus, said to his fellow disciples, We may as well go with him so that we can die alongside him. They were all afraid the leaders of the Jews would arrest and kill Jesus, for they did not yet understand the power of God.

5Now Jesus loved Martha, and her sister, and Lazarus. 6When he had heard therefore that he was sick, he abode two days still in the same place where he was. 7Then after that saith he to his disciples, Let us go into Judæa again. 8His disciples say unto him, Master, the Jews of late sought to stone thee; and goest thou thither again? 9Jesus answered, Are there not twelve hours in the day? If any man walk in the day, he stumbleth not, because he seeth the light of this world. 10But if a man walk in the night, he stumbleth, because there is no light in him. 11These things said he: and after that he saith unto them, Our friend Lazarus sleepeth; but I go, that I may awake him out of sleep. 12Then said his disciples, Lord, if he sleep, he shall do well. 13Howbeit Jesus spake of his death: but they thought that he had spoken of taking of rest in sleep. 14Then said Jesus unto them plainly, Lazarus is dead. 15And I am glad for your sakes that I was not there, to the intent ye may believe; nevertheless let us go unto him. 16Then said Thomas, which is called Didymus, unto his fellow disciples, Let us also go, that we may die with him.

3And when Jesus came to Martha's house in Bethany, Lazarus had already been in the grave four days. Now Bethany was near Jerusalem, less than two miles distant. There were many Jews at the house to mourn with Martha and Mary over their deceased brother. As soon as Martha heard that Jesus was coming and nearby, she hurried to meet him, but Mary remained in the house. Martha cried to Jesus, Lord, if you had been here my brother would not have died. But I know that even now whatever you ask of God, God will give you. Jesus said to her, Your brother will rise again. Martha replied to him, I know that he will rise again in the resurrection at the last day. Jesus said to her, I am the resurrection, and the life. He that believes in me, even though he were dead, yet will he live. And whoever lives and believes in me will never die, worlds without end. Do you believe this? She said to him, Yes, Lord. I believe you are the Messiah, the Son of God, who was foretold to come into the world.

4After this discussion, she quietly entered the house and told Mary to secretly leave with her. She said to her, Our Lord is here, and asking for you to meet with him. As soon as Mary heard that Jesus was there, she arose quickly and rushed out to meet him.

5Jesus had not yet arrived in the town, but was still at the place where Martha met him. The Jews in the house who were mourning with her, saw Mary abruptly depart and thought she was overcome with grief and was headed to

17Then when Jesus came, he found that he had lain in the grave four days already. 18Now Bethany was nigh unto Jerusalem, about fifteen furlongs off: 19And many of the Jews came to Martha and Mary, to comfort them concerning their brother. 20Then Martha, as soon as she heard that Jesus was coming, went and met him: but Mary sat still in the house. 21Then said Martha unto Jesus, Lord, if thou hadst been here, my brother had not died. 22But I know, that even now, whatsoever thou wilt ask of God, God will give it thee. 23Jesus saith unto her, Thy brother shall rise again. 24Martha saith unto him, I know that he shall rise again in the resurrection at the last day. 25Jesus said unto her, I am the resurrection, and the life: he that believeth in me, though he were dead, yet shall he live: 26And whosoever liveth and believeth in me shall never die. Believest thou this? 27She saith unto him, Yea, Lord: I believe that thou art the Christ, the Son of God, which should come into the world.

28And when she had so said, she went her way, and called Mary her sister secretly, saying, The Master is come, and calleth for thee. 29As soon as she heard that, she arose quickly, and came unto him.

30Now Jesus was not yet come into the town, but was in that place where Martha met him. 31The Jews then which were with her in the house, and comforted her, when they saw Mary, that she rose up hastily and went out, followed her,

the grave. They said, She is headed to the grave to weep and mourn there. When Mary arrived where Jesus was, and saw him, she fell down at his feet and said to him, Lord, if you had been here, my brother would not have died.

6Jesus looked upon her weeping, and the others who followed her also weeping, and he was grieved in his heart, and was troubled and said, Where have you laid his body? They told him, Lord, come and see. Jesus also wept. The Jews noticed and said, Look at how much he loved him! Some of them asked, Could not this man, who opened the eyes of the blind, have not also saved this man from dying? Hearing this Jesus again was grieved because of their misunderstanding.

7And he went to the grave. It was a burial cave, and had a stone blocking entry to it. Jesus said, Remove the stone blocking the cavern. Martha, the sister of the deceased man, said to him, Lord, by this time his decomposing body will stink because he has been dead for four days. Jesus reminded her, Did I not tell you that if you would believe you would behold God's glorious power? Then they removed the stone blocking the cave where the body lay. Then Jesus looked up to Heaven and said, Father, I thank you that you have heard me. I know you always listen to me, but I mention it for the benefit of those who are here witnessing this moment. Perhaps they will believe that I have been sent by you if they hear my prayer. Then with a loud voice Jesus commanded: Lazarus,

saying, She goeth unto the grave to weep there. 32Then when Mary was come where Jesus was, and saw him, she fell down at his feet, saying unto him, Lord, if thou hadst been here, my brother had not died.

33When Jesus therefore saw her weeping, and the Jews also weeping which came with her, he groaned in the spirit, and was troubled, 34And said, Where have ye laid him? They said unto him, Lord, come and see. 35Jesus wept. 36Then said the Jews, Behold how he loved him! 37And some of them said, Could not this man, which opened the eyes of the blind, have caused that even this man should not have died?

38Jesus therefore again groaning in himself cometh to the grave. It was a cave, and a stone lay upon it. 39Jesus said, Take ye away the stone. Martha, the sister of him that was dead, saith unto him, Lord, by this time he stinketh: for he hath been dead four days. 40Jesus saith unto her, Said I not unto thee, that, if thou wouldest believe, thou shouldest see the glory of God? 41Then they took away the stone from the place where the dead was laid. And Jesus lifted up his eyes, and said, Father, I thank thee that thou hast heard me. 42And I knew that thou hearest me always: but because of the people which stand by I said it, that they may believe that thou hast sent me. 43And when he thus had spoken, he cried with a loud voice, Lazarus, come forth. 44And he that was dead came

return to us from the grave. The man who was dead came out from the grave, his hands and feet still bound by grave-clothes, and his face covered with a burial shroud. Jesus instructed them, Untie him, and let him go.

⁸When the group of Jews who followed Mary saw what Jesus had done, most believed on him. But there were still some who immediately ran to the Pharisees to tell them what Jesus had just done.

⁹When they heard the report, the leaders summoned the Sanhedrin to meet, discussing the event and asking, What should we do? This man continues to do many miracles. If we ignore him and this continues, everyone will believe him, and the Romans will respond by taking away our right to lead, and will break apart our followers. A participant named Caiaphas, who was the high priest at that time, said to them, You understand nothing about how to deal with this threat to ourselves. It is better for one man to die to save our people than for our people to be lost. These words were inspired by God. Because he was the high priest at the time, he unwittingly spoke a true prophecy that Jesus would die to save those people. He would not merely save the Jews but also God's people throughout the world, whom he would gather as his family. From that moment the leaders determined on a plan to have Jesus killed.

¹⁰Jesus sensed their plan and avoided them. He traveled unseen

forth, bound hand and foot with graveclothes: and his face was bound about with a napkin. Jesus saith unto them, Loose him, and let him go.

⁴⁵Then many of the Jews which came to Mary, and had seen the things which Jesus did, believed on him. ⁴⁶But some of them went their ways to the Pharisees, and told them what things Jesus had done.

⁴⁷Then gathered the chief priests and the Pharisees a council, and said, What do we? for this man doeth many miracles. ⁴⁸If we let him thus alone, all men will believe on him: and the Romans shall come and take away both our place and nation. ⁴⁹And one of them, named Caiaphas, being the high priest that same year, said unto them, Ye know nothing at all, ⁵⁰Nor consider that it is expedient for us, that one man should die for the people, and that the whole nation perish not. ⁵¹And this spake he not of himself: but being high priest that year, he prophesied that Jesus should die for that nation; ⁵²And not for that nation only, but that also he should gather together in one the children of God that were scattered abroad. ⁵³Then from that day forth they took counsel together for to put him to death.

⁵⁴Jesus therefore walked no more openly among the Jews; but went

into the Judean wilderness to the city of Ephraim, where he and his followers remained undetected.

¹¹The time for the Jewish Passover arrived. Many people traveled up to Jerusalem before the Passover to participate in ceremonies to purify themselves. The leaders looked for Jesus to be there and asked members of the crowd standing in the temple, What do you think, will Jesus be coming to the Passover? There was standing direction from the Sanhedrin that if anyone saw Jesus in the city they were to tell the informants so that they could detain him.

¹²Six days before the Passover, Jesus returned to Bethany where he had raised Lazarus from the dead. They made supper for him and Martha served. Lazarus was among those who sat at the table with him. Many came to be there to see the man who was raised from the dead and to hear Jesus who had raised him.

¹³And among those who were present were his mother, and Mary, the Elect Lady who was companion with Jesus. She cut off the seven locks of his hair that had not been cut before because of the vow, which fell at her feet. This troubled his disciples who feared his strength would depart from him but said nothing because Jesus permitted it to be done. Jesus, seeing their concern, asked, Is not a lamb shorn before it is sacrificed? But they did not understand his meaning. And she took royal oil

thence unto a country near to the wilderness, into a city called Ephraim, and there continued with his disciples.

⁵⁵And the Jews' passover was nigh at hand: and many went out of the country up to Jerusalem before the passover, to purify themselves. ⁵⁶Then sought they for Jesus, and spake among themselves, as they stood in the temple, What think ye, that he will not come to the feast? ⁵⁷Now both the chief priests and the Pharisees had given a commandment, that, if any man knew where he were, he should shew it, that they might take him.

KJV Chapter 12

¹Then Jesus six days before the passover came to Bethany, where Lazarus was which had been dead, whom he raised from the dead.

²There they made him a supper; and Martha served: but Lazarus was one of them that sat at the table with him. ³Then took Mary a pound of ointment of spikenard, very costly, and anointed the feet of Jesus, and wiped his feet with her hair: and the house was filled with the odour of the ointment. ⁴Then saith one of his disciples, Judas Iscariot, Simon's son, which should betray him, ⁵Why was not this ointment sold for three hundred pence, and given to the poor? ⁶This he said, not that he cared for

used to coronate a king, containing spikenard, frankincense and myrrh, and applied it to the head, arms and hands, legs and feet of Jesus. And the house was filled with the smell of the royal anointing oil. One of his disciples, Judas Iscariot, Simon's son, who would later betray him, spoke up and asked, Why was this anointing oil wasted instead of sold for a year's wages of $40,000, and the money used to help the poor? He did not say this because he cared for the poor, but because he was a greedy thief who acted as treasurer for the group, and he wanted to get control over the money. Jesus rebuked him and said, Leave her alone. My mother has safeguarded this gift from my birth until now to be used for this moment. This anointing is required to be done to establish me before I lay down my life. The poor are always in need in this world, but I reign among you for only a short while and then am offered up as a sacrifice on your behalf.

the poor; but because he was a thief, and had the bag, and bare what was put therein. 7Then said Jesus, Let her alone: against the day of my burying hath she kept this. 8For the poor always ye have with you; but me ye have not always.

14Many of the Jews heard he had come to this dinner and came to see not only Jesus, but also to see Lazarus who had been raised from the dead. The Sanhedrin wanted Lazarus killed also, because raising him from the dead converted many people to believe Jesus was the Messiah.

9Much people of the Jews therefore knew that he was there: and they came not for Jesus' sake only, but that they might see Lazarus also, whom he had raised from the dead. 10But the chief priests consulted that they might put Lazarus also to death; 11Because that by reason of him many of the Jews went away, and believed on Jesus.

RE Chapter 9

1On the following day, many of those who were there for the Passover heard that Jesus would be entering Jerusalem. They took palm tree branches and went out to greet him as he entered, and

12On the next day much people that were come to the feast, when they heard that Jesus was coming to Jerusalem, 13Took branches of palm trees, and went forth to meet him, and cried, Hosanna: Blessed

shouted, Hosanna! Blessed is the King of Israel that comes in the name of the Lord.

²Jesus had sent two followers beforehand to get a young colt, and he entered Jerusalem riding on it. This was exactly what the prophet Zechariah foretold, Rejoice, daughter of Zion, shout out daughter of Jerusalem; behold, your King comes to you, he is just and provides salvation, meekly riding upon a young colt. At the time this happened, the disciples did not recognize that it was fulfilling prophecy, but after Jesus rose from the dead, then the disciples remembered the prophecy and how it had been fulfilled at that moment. The people who had been present when Lazarus was raised from the dead had spread word all over Jerusalem, and the welcoming crowd knew about that miracle and welcomed him into the city. The leaders were upset and said to each other, No one is following our direction. This whole population have become his followers!

³In the crowd that gathered for the Passover, there were certain Greeks who went to Philip, who was from Bethsaida of Galilee, and asked him, Sir, would you introduce us to Jesus? Philip went to tell Andrew, and together they went to tell Jesus that people were eager to meet him. And Jesus responded, The time has arrived when the Son of Man will complete his journey. In the name of Father Ahman I tell you, except a kernel of wheat is buried in the ground, it remains but a seed, but if it is buried, it can

is the King of Israel that cometh in the name of the Lord.

¹⁴And Jesus, when he had found a young ass, sat thereon; as it is written, ¹⁵Fear not, daughter of Sion: behold, thy King cometh, sitting on an ass's colt. ¹⁶These things understood not his disciples at the first: but when Jesus was glorified, then remembered they that these things were written of him, and that they had done these things unto him. ¹⁷The people therefore that was with him when he called Lazarus out of his grave, and raised him from the dead, bare record. ¹⁸For this cause the people also met him, for that they heard that he had done this miracle. ¹⁹The Pharisees therefore said among themselves, Perceive ye how ye prevail nothing? behold, the world is gone after him.

²⁰And there were certain Greeks among them that came up to worship at the feast: ²¹The same came therefore to Philip, which was of Bethsaida of Galilee, and desired him, saying, Sir, we would see Jesus. ²²Philip cometh and telleth Andrew: and again Andrew and Philip tell Jesus. ²³And Jesus answered them, saying, The hour is come, that the Son of man should be glorified. ²⁴Verily, verily, I say unto you, Except a corn of wheat fall into the ground and die, it abideth alone: but if it die, it

spring to life and bear fruit. Those who love their life will lose it, but those willing to sacrifice their life in this world will obtain endless lives, worlds without end. If any man is loyal to me, let him follow me and every upward step I achieve, there will my loyal followers join me. Any who are loyal to me, my Father will approve.

4Now I confront the final trial on my path, and what should I say? Father, save me from the difficulties I now face? When this is the reason I have come into the world. Father, let all honor be given to you. Then a voice from Heaven said, Every thing you have done has honored me, and every thing you will yet do will also honor me. The people nearby also heard the voice, but some thought it was thunder. Others thought an angel spoke to him. Jesus explained, You did not hear this voice for my benefit, but you heard it for your benefit. The time has come for me to complete the work required of me, to intercede for the world. And the accuser will lose all his power. Because of the sacrifice of his life that the Son of Man is to make, he will rise up and rescue all mankind. He said this to explain how important his death was to save others. The people who heard this asked him, When we consult the scriptures they claim that the Messiah will live forever. Why do you say the Son of Man must sacrifice his life? Who are you talking about? Then Jesus said to them, Only a little time remains for the light who is now here. Learn how to live while the light remains, otherwise darkness will overcome you. Without

bringeth forth much fruit. 25He that loveth his life shall lose it; and he that hateth his life in this world shall keep it unto life eternal. 26If any man serve me, let him follow me; and where I am, there shall also my servant be: if any man serve me, him will my Father honour.

27Now is my soul troubled; and what shall I say? Father, save me from this hour: but for this cause came I unto this hour. 28Father, glorify thy name. Then came there a voice from heaven, saying, I have both glorified it, and will glorify it again. 29The people therefore, that stood by, and heard it, said that it thundered: others said, An angel spake to him. 30Jesus answered and said, This voice came not because of me, but for your sakes. 31Now is the judgment of this world: now shall the prince of this world be cast out. 32And I, if I be lifted up from the earth, will draw all men unto me. 33This he said, signifying what death he should die. 34The people answered him, We have heard out of the law that Christ abideth for ever: and how sayest thou, The Son of man must be lifted up? who is this Son of man? 35Then Jesus said unto them, Yet a little while is the light with you. Walk while ye have the light, lest darkness come upon you: for he that walketh in darkness knoweth not whither he goeth. 36While ye have light, believe in the light, that ye may be the children of light. These things spake Jesus, and departed, and did hide himself from them.

the light you will fall into error. While you are near the light, believe in the light, so that you can become the children of light. Jesus said this, abruptly departed, and then avoided them.

5Although he had done many miracles before them, they still did not comprehend that he was the Messiah, fulfilling the prophecy of Isaiah about the Messiah, Who has believed our report? For whose benefit has the strength of the Lord been revealed? And Isaiah answered those questions by describing them: They will refuse to believe because Isaiah wrote, Make the heart of these people grow fat, dull their ears and shut their eyes, so they will not see with their eyes and hear with their ears, and understand with their heart, and repent, and be healed. Isaiah saw the Messiah's glory and prophesied of him.

37But though he had done so many miracles before them, yet they believed not on him: 38That the saying of Esaias the prophet might be fulfilled, which he spake, Lord, who hath believed our report? and to whom hath the arm of the Lord been revealed? 39Therefore they could not believe, because that Esaias said again, 40He hath blinded their eyes, and hardened their heart; that they should not see with their eyes, nor understand with their heart, and be converted, and I should heal them. 41These things said Esaias, when he saw his glory, and spake of him.

6Despite conflicts, some of the Sanhedrin also secretly believed on him. But because of the Pharisees they did not admit their belief, fearing they would be ejected from the synagogue, for they valued the praise of men more than the praise of God.

42Nevertheless among the chief rulers also many believed on him; but because of the Pharisees they did not confess him, lest they should be put out of the synagogue: 43For they loved the praise of men more than the praise of God.

7Jesus declared, He that believes on me, believes not just on me, but also on the one who sent me. What you see me do is what he that sent me has done before. I am here as the light of the world to enable anyone who believes on me to escape from the darkness. I do not judge those who hear my words, but do not believe, because I did not enter the world to now judge

44Jesus cried and said, He that believeth on me, believeth not on me, but on him that sent me. 45And he that seeth me seeth him that sent me. 46I am come a light into the world, that whosoever believeth on me should not abide in darkness. 47And if any man hear my words, and believe not, I judge him not: for I came not to judge the world, but to save the world. 48He

it, but to be its savior. But when you reject my message, beware, because the message I was sent by the Father to deliver will separate you in the last day. He will divide you based on your submission to, or rejection of, his message. He has sent me to guide you, and he guides into endless lives, worlds without end. My message, therefore, is the Father's.

that rejecteth me, and receiveth not my words, hath one that judgeth him: the word that I have spoken, the same shall judge him in the last day. ⁴⁹For I have not spoken of myself; but the Father which sent me, he gave me a commandment, what I should say, and what I should speak. ⁵⁰And I know that his commandment is life everlasting: whatsoever I speak therefore, even as the Father said unto me, so I speak.

RE Chapter 10

¹As the feast of the Passover approached, Jesus knew the time had arrived for his sacrificial death and return to the Father. He had loved and ministered to those who believed on him, and remained ministering to them until the end. At the conclusion of supper, Judas Iscariot, the son of Simon the leper, had been seduced by the accuser to betray Jesus.

²Jesus knew the Father had empowered him to have dominion over all things because he had been sent by the Father to redeem the world, then to return to the Father once he departed from the world. And so Jesus arose from supper and removed his cloak and took a towel as an apron. And he poured water into a basin, and he began to wash the disciples' feet and to dry them with the towel he wore as an apron. When he came to Simon Peter, Peter objected, saying, Lord, why do you wash my feet? Jesus answered and said to him, You will not understand this now, but will later come to understand this ordinance is necessary. Peter said to

KJV Chapter 13

¹Now before the feast of the passover, when Jesus knew that his hour was come that he should depart out of this world unto the Father, having loved his own which were in the world, he loved them unto the end. ²And supper being ended, the devil having now put into the heart of Judas Iscariot, Simon's son, to betray him;

³Jesus knowing that the Father had given all things into his hands, and that he was come from God, and went to God; ⁴He riseth from supper, and laid aside his garments; and took a towel, and girded himself. ⁵After that he poureth water into a basin, and began to wash the disciples' feet, and to wipe them with the towel wherewith he was girded. ⁶Then cometh he to Simon Peter: and Peter saith unto him, Lord, dost thou wash my feet? ⁷Jesus answered and said unto him, What I do thou knowest not now; but thou shalt know hereafter. ⁸Peter saith unto him, Thou shalt never wash my feet. Jesus answered him, If I wash thee not,

him, You do not need to wash my feet. Jesus answered him, If I do not wash your feet then you cannot rise up to be with me, for it is a required ordinance to be with me. Simon Peter still did not understand and said to him, Lord, if you must then don't just wash my feet, but finish the ordinance also on my hands and head. Jesus replied, Those whose hands and head have been washed only need to receive washing of their feet, and are clean from the blood and sins of this world. You whom I have washed today are clean, but not all of you. Now the ceremonies of the Jews under their law required them to wash, but Jesus washed for a higher purpose. And he knew who would betray him. Therefore he said, Not all of you are clean.

thou hast no part with me. 9Simon Peter saith unto him, Lord, not my feet only, but also my hands and my head. 10Jesus saith to him, He that is washed needeth not save to wash his feet, but is clean every whit: and ye are clean, but not all. 11For he knew who should betray him; therefore said he, Ye are not all clean.

3So after he had washed their feet and replaced his cloak and sat down again, he said to them, Do you understand the example I have just provided to you? You call me Master and Lord. And that is correct to say, for I am. If I am your Lord and Master, and knelt to wash your feet to cleanse you, you should also labor to make each other clean from the blood and sins of the world. For I have given you the example that you should do as I have done with you.

12So after he had washed their feet, and had taken his garments, and was set down again, he said unto them, Know ye what I have done to you? 13Ye call me Master and Lord: and ye say well; for so I am. 14If I then, your Lord and Master, have washed your feet; ye also ought to wash one another's feet. 15For I have given you an example, that ye should do as I have done to you.

4In the name of Father Ahman I declare to you, No servant is greater than his Lord, nor am I who have been sent greater than my Father, who sent me. Since you know these things, you will have joy if you follow them. I do not expect all of you to do as I have shown you. I know whom I have

16Verily, verily, I say unto you, The servant is not greater than his lord; neither he that is sent greater than he that sent him. 17If ye know these things, happy are ye if ye do them. 18I speak not of you all: I know whom I have chosen: but that the scripture may be fulfilled, He that eateth bread with me hath lifted

chosen, but the Psalm prophesies that my familiar and trusted friend, who ate bread with me, has lifted up his heel against me. I am telling you this beforehand so that when I am betrayed you do not lose your belief in me. I am the Messiah. In the name of Father Ahman I declare to you, He that accepts my word spoken by whomever I send with my word receives me, and he that receives me receives him that sent me, even my Father.

⁵When Jesus said this, he was troubled in spirit and declared, In the name of Father Ahman I say to you, one of you will betray me. Then the disciples looked at one another, wondering who he was talking about. One of the disciples Jesus loved was next to him at the table. Simon Peter got his attention and asked him to inquire of Jesus who he was referring to as a traitor. That disciple next to Jesus then asked him quietly, Lord, who is going to betray you? Jesus answered, It is the one to whom I will hand the bread I now dip. And when he had dipped the bread, he gave it to Judas Iscariot, the son of Simon. And he took the bread, at which point the accuser took control of Judas. Then Jesus said to him, What you have planned, do it quickly. Now no one at the table understood why he said this to him. For some of them thought that because Judas was the treasurer, Jesus was saying to him, Buy the things needed for the coming meal, or perhaps, he should give something to the poor. Judas, having received the bread, left immediately and entered the darkness.

up his heel against me. ¹⁹Now I tell you before it come, that, when it is come to pass, ye may believe that I am he. ²⁰Verily, verily, I say unto you, He that receiveth whomsoever I send receiveth me; and he that receiveth me receiveth him that sent me.

²¹When Jesus had thus said, he was troubled in spirit, and testified, and said, Verily, verily, I say unto you, that one of you shall betray me. ²²Then the disciples looked one on another, doubting of whom he spake. ²³Now there was leaning on Jesus' bosom one of his disciples, whom Jesus loved. ²⁴Simon Peter therefore beckoned to him, that he should ask who it should be of whom he spake. ²⁵He then lying on Jesus' breast saith unto him, Lord, who is it? ²⁶Jesus answered, He it is, to whom I shall give a sop, when I have dipped it. And when he had dipped the sop, he gave it to Judas Iscariot, the son of Simon. ²⁷And after the sop Satan entered into him. Then said Jesus unto him, That thou doest, do quickly. ²⁸Now no man at the table knew for what intent he spake this unto him. ²⁹For some of them thought, because Judas had the bag, that Jesus had said unto him, Buy those things that we have need of against the feast; or, that he should give something to the poor. ³⁰He then having received the sop went immediately out: and it was night.

6Then, after Judas had departed from them, Jesus said, Now is the Son of Man glorified, and God is glorified in him. If God is glorified through his sacrifice, God shall also glorify the one sacrificing himself and will never abandon him. Little children, I will only be with you a little while yet. You will want me here, but remember I said to the Jews, I will go onward on my path, and you will not take it with me. Now I tell you the same thing.

7I give you a new commandment, That you love one another. Love each other as I have loved you. If you have love for each other it will be a sign that will identify you to all mankind as my followers.

8Simon Peter asked him, Lord, where are you going? Jesus answered him, The steps I take next on the path, you will not be taking for now, but you will take those steps later on as you travel the same path. Peter responded to him, Lord, why can I not follow you right now? I am willing to lay down my life for you. Jesus answered him, Will you lay down your life for me? In the name of Father Ahman I tell you, The rooster will not crow tomorrow morning before you have denied me three times.

9Do not allow your heart to be troubled. You are devoted to God and are also devoted to me. In the journey through my Father's realms are many stages with temporary abodes. If it were not so, I would have told you. I go to prepare an abode for your upward journey. And when I arise, I will

31Therefore, when he was gone out, Jesus said, Now is the Son of man glorified, and God is glorified in him. 32If God be glorified in him, God shall also glorify him in himself, and shall straightway glorify him. 33Little children, yet a little while I am with you. Ye shall seek me: and as I said unto the Jews, Whither I go, ye cannot come; so now I say to you.

34A new commandment I give unto you, That ye love one another; as I have loved you, that ye also love one another. 35By this shall all men know that ye are my disciples, if ye have love one to another.

36Simon Peter said unto him, Lord, whither goest thou? Jesus answered him, Whither I go, thou canst not follow me now; but thou shalt follow me afterwards. 37Peter said unto him, Lord, why cannot I follow thee now? I will lay down my life for thy sake. 38Jesus answered him, Wilt thou lay down thy life for my sake? Verily, verily, I say unto thee, The cock shall not crow, till thou hast denied me thrice.

KJV Chapter 14

1Let not your heart be troubled: ye believe in God, believe also in me. 2In my Father's house are many mansions: if it were not so, I would have told you. I go to prepare a place for you. 3And if I go and prepare a place for you, I will come again, and receive you unto myself; that where I am, there ye may be

prepare places for you, but I will be your companion again and visit each of you, so that where I travel, you may journey to also. And the path I follow upward you know, and the way of ascent you also know. Thomas said to him, Lord, we don't know where you are going; how can we know the way? You have not told us. Jesus said to him, I am the way, the record of the truth, and the means for Eternal lives, worlds without end: no man comes to the Throne of the Father without me. If you follow me, you will come to the Father's Throne through me and will thereafter be like him forever.

10Philip said to him, Lord, reveal to us the Father and that will be all we ask. Jesus responded to him, Have I been with you this long and you still do not yet know who I am, Philip? Any who see me has seen my Father. How can you ask, Reveal to us the Father? Do you understand that I am in the Father, and the Father is in me? Do you understand that the words that I speak to you came from the Father, who is one with me? Nothing I have done is mine. Understand that the Father, who is one with me, is to be given credit for all I have done or will do. Believe me that I am one with the Father, and the Father is one with me; but if you do not, at least believe through these works. In the name of Father Ahman I declare to you, the individual who trusts me, what I have accomplished he will also. Followers will also accomplish the greater works I do next. Followers will also finish the path, as I am now concluding, at the place my Father

also. 4And whither I go ye know, and the way ye know. 5Thomas saith unto him, Lord, we know not whither thou goest; and how can we know the way? 6Jesus saith unto him, I am the way, the truth, and the life: no man cometh unto the Father, but by me. 7If ye had known me, ye should have known my Father also: and from henceforth ye know him, and have seen him.

8Philip saith unto him, Lord, shew us the Father, and it sufficeth us. 9Jesus saith unto him, Have I been so long time with you, and yet hast thou not known me, Philip? he that hath seen me hath seen the Father; and how sayest thou then, Shew us the Father? 10Believest thou not that I am in the Father, and the Father in me? the words that I speak unto you I speak not of myself: but the Father that dwelleth in me, he doeth the works. 11Believe me that I am in the Father, and the Father in me: or else believe me for the very works' sake. 12Verily, verily, I say unto you, He that believeth on me, the works that I do shall he do also; and greater works than these shall he do; because I go unto my Father. 13And whatsoever ye shall ask in my name, that will I do, that the Father may be glorified in the Son. 14If ye shall ask any thing in my name, I will do it.

dwells. As he helps me, I will help you, and you will accomplish what I have along with the greater sacrifice I have yet to finish. And whatever you shall ask in my name, I will answer, so that the Father may be glorified by the honor shown his Son. If you shall ask any thing in my name, I will answer.

11If you love me, stand ready, watching for every communication I will send to you. Remember that I will ask the Father, and he will provide to you another Comforter, that he may be by your side endlessly. You will obtain the record of Heaven, the truth of all things which is denied to the world because the world refuses my Father, and therefore they do not know him. But you know him, for he is with you, and shall provide answers to guide you. I will not leave you comfortless. I will stand at your side also.

12Yet a little while, and the world will no longer see me, but you will not lose sight of me because I give life, and you shall share in endless lives. You will know that I and the Father are one, and I am one with you, and you are one with me. He that treasures my teachings, and stands ready, watching for every communication I send him, is he who shows love for me. To those who show love for me, my Father will show love to them, and I love all those, and I will personally minister to them.

13Judas (not Iscariot), asked, Lord, how is it you will manifest yourself to us, but not to the world? Jesus answered and said to him, If a man

15If ye love me, keep my commandments. 16And I will pray the Father, and he shall give you another Comforter, that he may abide with you for ever; 17Even the Spirit of truth; whom the world cannot receive, because it seeth him not, neither knoweth him: but ye know him; for he dwelleth with you, and shall be in you. 18I will not leave you comfortless: I will come to you.

19Yet a little while, and the world seeth me no more; but ye see me: because I live, ye shall live also. 20At that day ye shall know that I am in my Father, and ye in me, and I in you. 21He that hath my commandments, and keepeth them, he it is that loveth me: and he that loveth me shall be loved of my Father, and I will love him, and will manifest myself to him.

22Judas saith unto him, not Iscariot, Lord, how is it that thou wilt manifest thyself unto us, and not unto the world? 23Jesus answered

loves me, he will stand ready, watching for every communication I will send to him; and my Father will also love him, and we will come visit him, and continually abide by his side.

¹⁴Whoever claims to love me but does not stand ready, watching for every communication I will send, indeed does not love me. These teachings are not from me, but come from the Father who sent me.

¹⁵These words have I spoken to you while I am still present with you. But the Comforter, which is the Holy Ghost that the Father will send in my name, will teach you all things, and restore to your memory all truth I have taught to you, and the record of Heaven itself.

¹⁶I leave you in peace, the peace only my teachings can provide for you and not as the world claims to find peace. Do not be confused nor fearful. You heard me say to you, I am leaving, and will return again. If you loved me, you would be rejoicing because I told you I am returning to my Father's realm. My Father dwells in the highest Heaven. I foretell you about what remains for me to accomplish so that you are not confused as it happens. When the coming events unfold I will not be able to explain it further as it occurs. The prince of darkness will not overcome me, but he can overcome you if you are confused and fearful. Remember, I explained that I will suffer because of my love for the Father, and he requires me to pass through this ordeal for your sakes, and I am

and said unto him, If a man love me, he will keep my words: and my Father will love him, and we will come unto him, and make our abode with him.

²⁴He that loveth me not keepeth not my sayings: and the word which ye hear is not mine, but the Father's which sent me.

²⁵These things have I spoken unto you, being yet present with you. ²⁶But the Comforter, which is the Holy Ghost, whom the Father will send in my name, he shall teach you all things, and bring all things to your remembrance, whatsoever I have said unto you.

²⁷Peace I leave with you, my peace I give unto you: not as the world giveth, give I unto you. Let not your heart be troubled, neither let it be afraid. ²⁸Ye have heard how I said unto you, I go away, and come again unto you. If ye loved me, ye would rejoice, because I said, I go unto the Father: for my Father is greater than I. ²⁹And now I have told you before it come to pass, that, when it is come to pass, ye might believe. ³⁰Hereafter I will not talk much with you: for the prince of this world cometh, and hath nothing in me. ³¹But that the world may know that I love the Father; and as the Father gave me commandment, even so I do. Arise, let us go hence.

ready to comply. Now let us walk together from this place.

17I am the true vine or head of the Father's family, and my Father is the husbandman over that family. Every branch connected to me that does not produce fruit, he will remove, and every branch that produces fruit he will prune back so that it produces better fruit. You will bear fruit if you follow the things I have taught you. Stay connected to me as part of the Heavenly family, and I will nourish you. Just as a branch cannot produce fruit if it is not connected to the vine, neither will you be able to bear fruit unless you remain connected with me. I am the vine, and you are the branches. He that stays connected to me, and I to him, will be abundantly fruitful; but without the connection to me you will perish. If a man loses his connection with me, he is merely a withered branch; and men take the withered branches, cut them away and burn them. If you stay connected to me, and my words live in you, you will ask according to my will, and you will be given the ability to accomplish my will. It will please and vindicate my Father if you produce abundant fruit, and that will prove you follow me. Just like the Father has loved me, I have in turn likewise loved you. Therefore, remain connected with me and my love will be with you. If you practice my teachings you will always remain connected with me; just as I have kept my Father's teachings and have remained connected with him.

KJV Chapter 15

1I am the true vine, and my Father is the husbandman. 2Every branch in me that beareth not fruit he taketh away: and every branch that beareth fruit, he purgeth it, that it may bring forth more fruit. 3Now ye are clean through the word which I have spoken unto you.

4Abide in me, and I in you. As the branch cannot bear fruit of itself, except it abide in the vine; no more can ye, except ye abide in me. 5I am the vine, ye are the branches: He that abideth in me, and I in him, the same bringeth forth much fruit: for without me ye can do nothing. 6If a man abide not in me, he is cast forth as a branch, and is withered; and men gather them, and cast them into the fire, and they are burned. 7If ye abide in me, and my words abide in you, ye shall ask what ye will, and it shall be done unto you.

8Herein is my Father glorified, that ye bear much fruit; so shall ye be my disciples. 9As the Father hath loved me, so have I loved you: continue ye in my love. 10If ye keep my commandments, ye shall abide in my love; even as I have kept my Father's commandments, and abide in his love.

18I say these things to you so I will be able to rejoice at your triumph. You will overcome all obstacles if you follow what I have taught.

19This is my commandment: That you love one another as I have loved you. No man loves more than when he is willing to sacrifice his life to save his friends. You are my friends if you do whatever I communicate to you. Beginning now, I will no longer call you my servants because a servant does not share his Lord's life. But I make you my friends because every thing I received from my Father I have shared and will yet share with you. You did not choose me, but I have chosen you, and ordained you, that you should progress and become fruitful, that your fruit will testify on your behalf forever, that whatever I direct you to seek from my Father you will be able to obtain. I have taught these things to you to enable you to share my love among one another.

20The world will hate you, but you know that it hated me before it hates you. If you belonged to the world, the world would love its property. But because you are not a captive of the world, and I have freed you from the world, the world hates you.

21Remember that I told you before that no servant is greater than his Lord. If many have persecuted me, many will also persecute you, but if some few have followed my teachings, some few will follow yours also. The world's response to you will be because you will act in my name and on my behalf. Those

11These things have I spoken unto you, that my joy might remain in you, and that your joy might be full.

12This is my commandment, That ye love one another, as I have loved you. 13Greater love hath no man than this, that a man lay down his life for his friends. 14Ye are my friends, if ye do whatsoever I command you. 15Henceforth I call you not servants; for the servant knoweth not what his lord doeth: but I have called you friends; for all things that I have heard of my Father I have made known unto you. 16Ye have not chosen me, but I have chosen you, and ordained you, that ye should go and bring forth fruit, and that your fruit should remain: that whatsoever ye shall ask of the Father in my name, he may give it you. 17These things I command you, that ye love one another.

18If the world hate you, ye know that it hated me before it hated you. 19If ye were of the world, the world would love his own: but because ye are not of the world, but I have chosen you out of the world, therefore the world hateth you.

20Remember the word that I said unto you, The servant is not greater than his lord. If they have persecuted me, they will also persecute you; if they have kept my saying, they will keep yours also. 21But all these things will they do unto you for my name's sake, because they know not him that sent

who fight against you are strangers to my Father. If I had not come and testified of the truth to them, they would not be accountable for rebellion, but now they have no excuse for their rebellion. If they hate me, they hate my Father also. If I had not shown to them an example no other man has shown before, they would not be accountable. But they have rebelled after seeing with their own eyes and hearing with their ears the one sent by Father Ahman to them, and have rebelled against us both. Proving men in this way fulfills the prophecy, They hated me without a cause.

22As for you, when the Comforter comes (or in other words the Spirit of truth emanating from my Father), that spirit will testify of me. Then you have the ability to also testify of me. This is because you have followed me from the beginning or before the world was organized.

23Now I tell you beforehand what to expect to come upon you so you are not surprised, nor will you stumble and fall. They will excommunicate you. The time will even come that the self-righteous who kill you will think that they speak for God. And they will do these things because they cannot do what the Father and I have done. I warn you beforehand that you will face this opposition so that when it happens you will remember and be strengthened. When I first taught, the anger and opposition was directed at me, and because of that, you were not their focus. But now I will return to the

me. 22If I had not come and spoken unto them, they had not had sin: but now they have no cloak for their sin. 23He that hateth me hateth my Father also. 24If I had not done among them the works which none other man did, they had not had sin: but now have they both seen and hated both me and my Father. 25But this cometh to pass, that the word might be fulfilled that is written in their law, They hated me without a cause.

26But when the Comforter is come, whom I will send unto you from the Father, even the Spirit of truth, which proceedeth from the Father, he shall testify of me: 27And ye also shall bear witness, because ye have been with me from the beginning.

KJV Chapter 16

1These things have I spoken unto you, that ye should not be offended. 2They shall put you out of the synagogues: yea, the time cometh, that whosoever killeth you will think that he doeth God service. 3And these things will they do unto you, because they have not known the Father, nor me. 4But these things have I told you, that when the time shall come, ye may remember that I told you of them. And these things I said not unto you at the beginning, because I was with you.

one who sent me and they will turn their anger at you.

24I said that I return to the one who sent me and none of you asked me to explain what I meant by that. Instead you have become saddened and downhearted. Understand this truth from me: It is for your benefit that I ascend to the Father. If I do not take up my position there I cannot send the spirit of truth, the record of Heaven, the peaceable things of immortal glory to lead you upward. Once I ascend to the Father, I will send the Comforter to guide you on the upward path. The light is given to shine upon the pathway, to expose wrongdoing, and let you decide matters correctly. Those who refused to become devoted to me will not receive this. Because I will ascend to the Father, you will be guided, and they who follow the adversary will be rejected with the adversary they follow. He has already been rejected by the Father.

25There are many things I still have to teach you, but you are not able to understand it all as yet. When I am the Spirit of Truth, I can then reveal to you the record of Heaven and knowledge will be poured into you. The spirit is the means to communicate my words, and my words will lead you on the upward path. The knowledge poured in to you will come from me. I will depart, but only briefly because when I ascend back to the Head of the Household of Heaven, I will also be by your side to guide you by my voice from Heaven.

5But now I go my way to him that sent me; and none of you asketh me, Whither goest thou? 6But because I have said these things unto you, sorrow hath filled your heart. 7Nevertheless I tell you the truth; It is expedient for you that I go away: for if I go not away, the Comforter will not come unto you; but if I depart, I will send him unto you. 8And when he is come, he will reprove the world of sin, and of righteousness, and of judgment: 9Of sin, because they believe not on me; 10Of righteousness, because I go to my Father, and ye see me no more; 11Of judgment, because the prince of this world is judged.

12I have yet many things to say unto you, but ye cannot bear them now. 13Howbeit when he, the Spirit of truth, is come, he will guide you into all truth: for he shall not speak of himself; but whatsoever he shall hear, that shall he speak: and he will shew you things to come. 14He shall glorify me: for he shall receive of mine, and shall shew it unto you. 15All things that the Father hath are mine: therefore said I, that he shall take of mine, and shall shew it unto you. 16A little while, and ye shall not see me: and again, a little while, and ye shall see me, because I go to the Father.

26Then some of his disciples questioned among themselves, What does he mean he will depart briefly, then when he has ascended to the Father he will be by our side? What do these words mean? We do not understand.

27Now Jesus knew that they wanted to ask him to explain and said to them, Do you discuss among yourselves what I meant when I said, I will depart, but only briefly, because when I ascend back to the Father, I will be by your side to guide you by my voice from Heaven? In the name of Father Ahman I forewarn you, You will grieve and mourn, but that will turn to joy and rejoicing. When a woman is in labor she suffers because the time to give birth has come, but after the child is born she forgets the pain and is joyful over her newborn child. You will mourn my departure, and celebrate my return, and that joy will never leave you. Then you will not need to ask of me, but you should ask Father Ahman in my name for what is needed. From now on, inquire from Father Ahman using my name and you will always receive an answer.

28Much of what I have said to you may seem like a riddle, but the time will come when you will comprehend my words and they will no longer seem a riddle, and you will understand them plainly. When I ascend and you ask the Father in my name, you will know

17Then said some of his disciples among themselves, What is this that he saith unto us, A little while, and ye shall not see me: and again, a little while, and ye shall see me: and, Because I go to the Father? 18They said therefore, What is this that he saith, A little while? we cannot tell what he saith.

19Now Jesus knew that they were desirous to ask him, and said unto them, Do ye inquire among yourselves of that I said, A little while, and ye shall not see me: and again, a little while, and ye shall see me? 20Verily, verily, I say unto you, That ye shall weep and lament, but the world shall rejoice: and ye shall be sorrowful, but your sorrow shall be turned into joy. 21A woman when she is in travail hath sorrow, because her hour is come: but as soon as she is delivered of the child, she remembereth no more the anguish, for joy that a man is born into the world. 22 And ye now therefore have sorrow: but I will see you again, and your heart shall rejoice, and your joy no man taketh from you. 23And in that day ye shall ask me nothing. Verily, verily, I say unto you, Whatsoever ye shall ask the Father in my name, he will give it you. 24Hitherto have ye asked nothing in my name: ask, and ye shall receive, that your joy may be full.

25These things have I spoken unto you in proverbs: but the time cometh, when I shall no more speak unto you in proverbs, but I shall shew you plainly of the Father. 26At that day ye shall ask in my name: and I say not unto you, that I will pray the Father for you:

that Father Ahman loves you because you have been devoted to me, and have accepted that I came from the Head of the Household of Heaven and was sent by him into the world, and that I will return to be with him.

²⁹His disciples said unto him, Very good, now you are making it clear and not using a riddle. We are certain that you did come from the Father and were sent by him. Jesus answered them, At this moment you are truly committed in this belief, but the time is quickly upon us when you will scatter in fear and leave me alone to face the adversary. Even without you I will never be alone, because the Father remains with me in every trial here. I tell you this beforehand so you will be reassured. In this world there are difficult trials to be faced by my followers, but those who remain devoted will, like me, finish the path and experience the fullness of joy.

³⁰Then Jesus looked up to Heaven and said these words, Father, the hour has arrived. Let your light abide with your Son, that your Son may be filled by your light and illuminate others. Because you have taught me to overcome the weaknesses of the flesh, you guide me to gain power to heal all weaknesses and redeem all creation. From your presence come Eternal lives, worlds without end, and you are the sole source of all truth. Therefore, it is known and will be known that I am the Messiah sent by you. I have kept every obligation you have asked of me and now

²⁷For the Father himself loveth you, because ye have loved me, and have believed that I came out from God. ²⁸I came forth from the Father, and am come into the world: again, I leave the world, and go to the Father.

²⁹His disciples said unto him, Lo, now speakest thou plainly, and speakest no proverb. ³⁰Now are we sure that thou knowest all things, and needest not that any man should ask thee: by this we believe that thou camest forth from God. ³¹Jesus answered them, Do ye now believe? ³²Behold, the hour cometh, yea, is now come, that ye shall be scattered, every man to his own, and shall leave me alone: and yet I am not alone, because the Father is with me. ³³These things I have spoken unto you, that in me ye might have peace. In the world ye shall have tribulation: but be of good cheer; I have overcome the world.

KJV Chapter 17

¹These words spake Jesus, and lifted up his eyes to heaven, and said, Father, the hour is come; glorify thy Son, that thy Son also may glorify thee: ²As thou hast given him power over all flesh, that he should give eternal life to as many as thou hast given him. ³And this is life eternal, that they might know thee the only true God, and Jesus Christ, whom thou hast sent. ⁴I have glorified thee on the earth: I have finished the work which thou gavest me to do. ⁵ And now, O Father, glorify thou me with thine own self with the glory which I

have completed this part of the work. Let what happens next finish your great work, so I may return to your Throne to be with you where I was before my descent here.

had with thee before the world was.

31I have explained your title to the men you gave to me from out of the fallen creation. They were yours at the beginning, and you have given them to me as my offspring. And they are devoted, prepared and always waiting to respond to your words. Now they understand and accept that every thing I have done and taught comes from you. For I have said to them the things you told to me. They are devoted to the truth and know I am your sent Messiah. I pray for them, and what I ask is for them and not the world, for they are yours. And all who are devoted to me are yours, and you share with me, and I am their light. I am soon to depart from this creation, but these followers will remain here as I return again to be with you. Holy Father, please watch over these like a sentinel. Protect and guard them using your power, so that they may be united as one, as we are united as one. While I accompanied them in the world, I shared light with them in your name. Every one you gave to me I have kept, and none of them will be lost to us, other than the son of perdition. Those who are kept and those who are lost are divided according to your covenant made from the beginning.

6I have manifested thy name unto the men which thou gavest me out of the world: thine they were, and thou gavest them me; and they have kept thy word. 7Now they have known that all things whatsoever thou hast given me are of thee. 8For I have given unto them the words which thou gavest me; and they have received them, and have known surely that I came out from thee, and they have believed that thou didst send me. 9I pray for them: I pray not for the world, but for them which thou hast given me; for they are thine. 10And all mine are thine, and thine are mine; and I am glorified in them. 11And now I am no more in the world, but these are in the world, and I come to thee. Holy Father, keep through thine own name those whom thou hast given me, that they may be one, as we are. 12While I was with them in the world, I kept them in thy name: those that thou gavest me I have kept, and none of them is lost, but the son of perdition; that the scripture might be fulfilled.

32And now I will be returning to you, and I declare these words in the world so these devoted believ-

13And now come I to thee; and these things I speak in the world, that they might have my joy ful-

ers can share in my coming joyful triumph. I have taught them your word, and the world rejects them because they are not taken in by worldliness, even as I am not distracted by the world. I do not ask for you to remove them from the coming challenges here, but protect them from falling prey to temptations of worldliness. They are not worldly, even as I am not. Sanctify them through your truth. Your words are truth. As you have sent me into the world, likewise I am sending them into the world. And for their sakes I sacrifice myself, that they might be sanctified through the truth.

33I pray not only for these followers, but also for all believers who learn our words from them. I ask that all followers and believers may be united as one, as you, Father, are in me, and I am in you, that they also may be united as one in us. By them becoming one, the world will have reason to believe that you sent me. And the light which you gave to me I have given to them. This allows them to become united as one, even as we are one: my light in them, and your light in me. The light will lead them to be made perfect in one. That light I have given to them is evidence to the world that you have sent me. I have loved them, as you have loved me. Father, I ask that those whom you have given to me may also ascend to live where I am ascending, for this journey was established before the foundation of creation. O righteous Father, this fallen world does not know you, but I have declared that you have sent me to minister here. I

filled in themselves. 14I have given them thy word; and the world hath hated them, because they are not of the world, even as I am not of the world. 15I pray not that thou shouldest take them out of the world, but that thou shouldest keep them from the evil. 16They are not of the world, even as I am not of the world. 17Sanctify them through thy truth: thy word is truth. 18As thou hast sent me into the world, even so have I also sent them into the world. 19And for their sakes I sanctify myself, that they also might be sanctified through the truth.

20Neither pray I for these alone, but for them also which shall believe on me through their word; 21That they all may be one; as thou, Father, art in me, and I in thee, that they also may be one in us: that the world may believe that thou hast sent me. 22And the glory which thou gavest me I have given them; that they may be one, even as we are one: 23I in them, and thou in me, that they may be made perfect in one; and that the world may know that thou hast sent me, and hast loved them, as thou hast loved me.

24Father, I will that they also, whom thou hast given me, be with me where I am; that they may behold my glory, which thou hast given me: for thou lovedst me before the foundation of the world. 25O righteous Father, the world hath not known thee: but I have known thee, and these have known that thou hast sent me. 26And I have declared unto them thy

have declared your message here and will finish the course. May the love you have for me be shown through the example of my love for them, and they may be saved through my sacrifice.

name, and will declare it: that the love wherewith thou hast loved me may be in them, and I in them.

RE Chapter 11

¹When Jesus had spoken these words, he took his disciples and walked across the Cedron brook, where there was a garden that he and his disciples entered. And there he worked wondrously, his disciples being overcome with awe, collapsed to the ground.

²Jesus had often visited this garden, and Judas knew of the place. Judas led a party under orders by the Sanhedrin, carrying lanterns, torches and weapons. Jesus knew what would happen, and confronted the armed party asking, Who are you looking for? They answered, Jesus of Nazareth. He declared, I am that I am! Hearing this bold claim startled the Sanhedrin's armed men, and they tripped over one another when they took a surprised step backwards. Jesus asked again, Who are you looking for? (to require them to acknowledge by their own voice that he was the God of Israel). And they said, Jesus of Nazareth. Jesus answered, I have told you that I am!

³Jesus said, If you are looking for me, then let these others go on their way. This request was to fulfill his prophecy, Every one you gave to me I have kept, and none of them will be lost to us.

KJV Chapter 18

¹When Jesus had spoken these words, he went forth with his disciples over the brook Cedron, where was a garden, into the which he entered, and his disciples.

²And Judas also, which betrayed him, knew the place: for Jesus ofttimes resorted thither with his disciples. ³Judas then, having received a band of men and officers from the chief priests and Pharisees, cometh thither with lanterns and torches and weapons. ⁴Jesus therefore, knowing all things that should come upon him, went forth, and said unto them, Whom seek ye? ⁵They answered him, Jesus of Nazareth. Jesus saith unto them, I am he. And Judas also, which betrayed him, stood with them. ⁶As soon then as he had said unto them, I am he, they went backward, and fell to the ground. ⁷Then asked he them again, Whom seek ye? And they said, Jesus of Nazareth. ⁸Jesus answered, I have told you that I am he:

if therefore ye seek me, let these go their way: ⁹That the saying might be fulfilled, which he spake, Of them which thou gavest me have I lost none.

4Then Simon Peter had a sword and drew it, and struck the high priest's servant and cut off his right ear. The servant's name was Malchus, who later believed on Jesus. Then Jesus said to Peter, Put your sword back in the sheath. The cup my Father has given to me, should I refuse to drink it?

5Then the party under orders from the Sanhedrin took Jesus, and bound him. And they led him away first to Annas, the father-in-law of Caiaphas, who was the high priest during that year. Now Caiaphas was the same man who counseled that it is better for one man to die to save the people than for the people to be lost.

6Simon Peter followed behind Jesus, and so did a second disciple who was familiar to the high priest and was permitted access to enter the high priest's house. But Peter remained outside by the door. After entry, the second disciple returned and spoke to the doorkeeper and gained access for Peter to enter the house also. The doorkeeper asked Peter, Aren't you one of the accused man's followers? He answered, No I am not. And there were members of the party who brought Jesus back who were warming themselves beside a coal fire, and Peter was also cold so he warmed himself beside them.

7The high priest questioned Jesus about the identities of his followers and about his doctrine. And Jesus answered him, I spoke boldly to everyone. I taught frequently in the synagogue and in the temple,

10Then Simon Peter having a sword drew it, and smote the high priest's servant, and cut off his right ear. The servant's name was Malchus. 11Then said Jesus unto Peter, Put up thy sword into the sheath: the cup which my Father hath given me, shall I not drink it?

12Then the band and the captain and officers of the Jews took Jesus, and bound him, 13And led him away to Annas first; for he was father in law to Caiaphas, which was the high priest that same year. 14Now Caiaphas was he, which gave counsel to the Jews, that it was expedient that one man should die for the people.

15And Simon Peter followed Jesus, and so did another disciple: that disciple was known unto the high priest, and went in with Jesus into the palace of the high priest. 16But Peter stood at the door without. Then went out that other disciple, which was known unto the high priest, and spake unto her that kept the door, and brought in Peter. 17Then saith the damsel that kept the door unto Peter, Art not thou also one of this man's disciples? He saith, I am not. 18And the servants and officers stood there, who had made a fire of coals; for it was cold: and they warmed themselves: and Peter stood with them, and warmed himself.

19The high priest then asked Jesus of his disciples, and of his doctrine. 20Jesus answered him, I spake openly to the world; I ever taught in the synagogue, and in the temple, whither the Jews always re-

where the Jews are present to hear. I have made no attempt to be secret. Why ask me these questions? Ask the many people who heard me teach and they can tell you what I said; they know. After he said this, one of the men holding Jesus hit him with his palm and said, Do you dare to speak to the high priest that way? Jesus responded to him, If I have spoken like an evil sorcerer, testify of the sorcery, but if not, why did you strike me? Annas then had him taken in the bindings and brought to Caiaphas, the high priest.

8As Simon Peter stood and warmed himself, the people standing by the fire asked him, Are you not one of his followers? He denied it, and said, No I am not. One of the servants of the high priest who was related to the man whose ear Peter had cut off then asked, Did I not see you in the garden with him? Peter then denied again, and immediately the crowing of a rooster sounded.

9Then they led Jesus from Caiaphas to the Roman judgment hall, and it was still before sunrise. The Sanhedrin did not enter the judgment hall because it would defile them and prevent them from participating in the Passover. Pilate came out and confronted them and asked, What accusation do you have against this man? They answered and said to him, Would we bring him to you if he were not a sorcerer? Then Pilate said to them, That is no Roman concern. You take him, and judge him against your own law. The Jews therefore said to him, We do

sort; and in secret have I said nothing. 21Why askest thou me? ask them which heard me, what I have said unto them: behold, they know what I said. 22And when he had thus spoken, one of the officers which stood by struck Jesus with the palm of his hand, saying, Answerest thou the high priest so? 23Jesus answered him, If I have spoken evil, bear witness of the evil: but if well, why smitest thou me? 24Now Annas had sent him bound unto Caiaphas the high priest.

25And Simon Peter stood and warmed himself. They said therefore unto him, Art not thou also one of his disciples? He denied it, and said, I am not. 26One of the servants of the high priest, being his kinsman whose ear Peter cut off, saith, Did not I see thee in the garden with him? 27Peter then denied again: and immediately the cock crew.

28Then led they Jesus from Caiaphas unto the hall of judgment: and it was early; and they themselves went not into the judgment hall, lest they should be defiled; but that they might eat the passover. 29Pilate then went out unto them, and said, What accusation bring ye against this man? 30They answered and said unto him, If he were not a malefactor, we would not have delivered him up unto thee. 31Then said Pilate unto them, Take ye him, and judge him according to your law. The Jews therefore said unto him, It is not lawful for us to put any man to

not crucify a man on the Passover under our tradition, referring to the prophecy Jesus had spoken about the kind of execution he would suffer.

¹⁰Then Pilate stepped back into the judgment hall and addressed Jesus and said to him, You are the King of the Jews? Jesus answered him, Did you say this to me on your own, or did others tell you to say it to me? Pilate answered, Am I a Jew? Your own people and the chief priests have turned you over to me. How do you justify yourself? Jesus answered, My kingdom is not of this world. If my kingdom were of this world, then my followers would fight to prevent the Jews from taking me as their captive. But my kingdom is not comprised of the Jews. Pilate responded, So you admit you claim to be a King? Jesus replied, It was you that just said I was a king. The reason I was sent into this world was to be a witness of the truth. Every person who is loyal to the truth listens to my teachings. Pilate responded to him, What is truth? And after saying this, he went out again to the Jews and said to them, I find no reason to punish him. You have asked me for clemency for a Jewish prisoner to respect your Passover; shall I free your King of the Jews? They all shouted out, Not this man, but Barabbas. Now Barabbas was a robber.

¹¹Then Pilate had his guards take Jesus and beat him. And the soldiers put on his head a crown of

death: ³²That the saying of Jesus might be fulfilled, which he spake, signifying what death he should die.

³³Then Pilate entered into the judgment hall again, and called Jesus, and said unto him, Art thou the King of the Jews? ³⁴Jesus answered him, Sayest thou this thing of thyself, or did others tell it thee of me? ³⁵Pilate answered, Am I a Jew? Thine own nation and the chief priests have delivered thee unto me: what hast thou done? ³⁶Jesus answered, My kingdom is not of this world: if my kingdom were of this world, then would my servants fight, that I should not be delivered to the Jews: but now is my kingdom not from hence. ³⁷Pilate therefore said unto him, Art thou a king then? Jesus answered, Thou sayest that I am a king. To this end was I born, and for this cause came I into the world, that I should bear witness unto the truth. Every one that is of the truth heareth my voice. ³⁸Pilate saith unto him, What is truth? And when he had said this, he went out again unto the Jews, and saith unto them, I find in him no fault at all. ³⁹But ye have a custom, that I should release unto you one at the passover: will ye therefore that I release unto you the King of the Jews? ⁴⁰Then cried they all again, saying, Not this man, but Barabbas. Now Barabbas was a robber.

KJV Chapter 19

¹Then Pilate therefore took Jesus, and scourged him. ²And the soldiers plaited a crown of thorns,

acanthus, and they dressed him in a purple robe and said, Hail, King of the Jews! and they hit him and made sport of him. Pilate thereafter went back out, and said to the Jewish leaders, Behold, I bring him back to you, that you may know that I find no reason to punish him any further. Then Jesus came out wearing the crown of acanthus and the purple robe. And Pilate said to them, Behold the man!

12When the chief priests and leaders saw him, they cried out saying, Crucify him! Crucify him! Pilate said to them, You take him and you crucify him, for I have no quarrel against him. The Jews answered him, We have a law, and our law imposes the death penalty because he blasphemed by falsely claiming to be the Son of God.

13When Pilate heard them say that, he was alarmed, and he returned with Jesus into the judgment hall and asked him, Who are you? But Jesus did not answer. Then Pilate said to him, Do you refuse to speak to me? Do you not realize that I have the power of life and death? Jesus answered, You have no authority over me except that permitted by Heaven. Those who handed me over to you have the greatest sin. Pilate decided then that he would release him of any charge, but the Jews shouted, If you let this man go you are not loyal to Caesar. When anyone claims to be a king he commits treason against Caesar. When Pilate heard that accusation, he brought Jesus out and sat down in the judgment seat in a place called the Pavement; in Hebrew called

and put it on his head, and they put on him a purple robe, 3And said, Hail, King of the Jews! and they smote him with their hands. 4Pilate therefore went forth again, and saith unto them, Behold, I bring him forth to you, that ye may know that I find no fault in him. 5Then came Jesus forth, wearing the crown of thorns, and the purple robe. And Pilate saith unto them, Behold the man!

6When the chief priests therefore and officers saw him, they cried out, saying, Crucify him, crucify him. Pilate saith unto them, Take ye him, and crucify him: for I find no fault in him. 7The Jews answered him, We have a law, and by our law he ought to die, because he made himself the Son of God.

8When Pilate therefore heard that saying, he was the more afraid; 9And went again into the judgment hall, and saith unto Jesus, Whence art thou? But Jesus gave him no answer. 10Then saith Pilate unto him, Speakest thou not unto me? knowest thou not that I have power to crucify thee, and have power to release thee? 11Jesus answered, Thou couldest have no power at all against me, except it were given thee from above: therefore he that delivered me unto thee hath the greater sin. 12And from thenceforth Pilate sought to release him: but the Jews cried out, saying, If thou let this man go, thou art not Cæsar's friend: whosoever maketh himself a king speaketh against Cæsar. 13When Pilate therefore heard that saying, he brought Jesus forth, and sat

Gabbatha. At the time it was approaching mid-day, time to begin to prepare the Passover feast. Pilate announced to the Jews, Behold your King! But they shouted back, Take him away and crucify him. Pilate said to them, Shall I crucify your King? The Jewish leaders declared, We have no king but Caesar. We will crucify him ourselves. And Pilate turned him over to those who were going to crucify him, sending but one soldier to accompany them with a plaque he ordered to be displayed.

14And they took Jesus, and led him away. And he carried his cross and was taken to a place called the place of the skull, which had the Hebrew name Golgotha. Here the leaders directed his crucifixion, and two others who had been crucified by the Romans were also there at the same time, one on either side, with Jesus in the middle. When Pilate surrendered Jesus to be crucified, he had a plaque prepared in Hebrew, Greek and Latin to be displayed on the cross. The plaque announced: Jesus of Nazareth the King of the Jews. This announcement was read by many of the passing Jews. For the place where Jesus was crucified was beside the city road and many pilgrims were walking by. Then the chief priests of the Jews complained to Pilate, Either take it down or do not write: The King of the Jews. Instead write that he claimed, I am King of the Jews. Pilate answered, That which I have written I have written.

15Now the guards, when they had crucified Jesus, took his garments

down in the judgment seat in a place that is called the Pavement, but in the Hebrew, Gabbatha. 14And it was the preparation of the passover, and about the sixth hour: and he saith unto the Jews, Behold your King! 15But they cried out, Away with him, away with him, crucify him. Pilate saith unto them, Shall I crucify your King? The chief priests answered, We have no king but Cæsar. 16Then delivered he him therefore unto them to be crucified.

And they took Jesus, and led him away. 17 And he bearing his cross went forth into a place called the place of a skull, which is called in the Hebrew Golgotha: 18Where they crucified him, and two other with him, on either side one, and Jesus in the midst. 19And Pilate wrote a title, and put it on the cross. And the writing was, JESUS OF NAZARETH THE KING OF THE JEWS. 20This title then read many of the Jews: for the place where Jesus was crucified was nigh to the city: and it was written in Hebrew, and Greek, and Latin. 21Then said the chief priests of the Jews to Pilate, Write not, The King of the Jews; but that he said, I am King of the Jews. 22Pilate answered, What I have written I have written.

23Then the soldiers, when they had crucified Jesus, took his garments, and made four parts, to every guard a part; and also his coat. The coat was without seam, woven from the top throughout. They agreed among themselves, Let us not cut it up, but cast lots for it, and someone will take it whole. This fulfilled the prophecy in scripture that foretold, They parted my raiment among them, and for my vesture they did cast lots. This prophecy foretold how the guards would divide his raiment as he was dying.

16Now remaining at the cross with Jesus were his mother, and his aunt, and Mary the wife of Cleophas, and Mary the Elect Lady. When Jesus saw his mother and the beloved disciple standing together, he said to his mother, Woman, behold your son! Then he said to the disciple, Behold your mother! And from that hour that disciple accepted her as part of his own household.

17After this, Jesus knowing that every thing had been fully accomplished to fulfill prophecy said, I thirst. Now there was a vessel full of vinegar, mixed with gall. They dipped a sponge into it and using a hyssop branch raised it to his mouth. When Jesus had received the vinegar, he said, My path is completed! Then he bowed his head and entrusted his spirit back to the Father.

18The Jews were concerned about preparations for the Passover, and did not want crucifixions to continue into the Holy Day. Therefore they inquired of Pilate to find if he would object if they had the legs of

and made four parts, to every soldier a part; and also his coat: now the coat was without seam, woven from the top throughout. 24They said therefore among themselves, Let us not rend it, but cast lots for it, whose it shall be: that the scripture might be fulfilled, which saith, They parted my raiment among them, and for my vesture they did cast lots. These things therefore the soldiers did.

25Now there stood by the cross of Jesus his mother, and his mother's sister, Mary the wife of Cleophas, and Mary Magdalene. 26When Jesus therefore saw his mother, and the disciple standing by, whom he loved, he saith unto his mother, Woman, behold thy son! 27Then saith he to the disciple, Behold thy mother! And from that hour that disciple took her unto his own home.

28After this, Jesus knowing that all things were now accomplished, that the scripture might be fulfilled, saith, I thirst. 29Now there was set a vessel full of vinegar: and they filled a sponge with vinegar, and put it upon hyssop, and put it to his mouth. 30When Jesus therefore had received the vinegar, he said, It is finished: and he bowed his head, and gave up the ghost.

31The Jews therefore, because it was the preparation, that the bodies should not remain upon the cross on the sabbath day, (for that sabbath day was an high day,) besought Pilate that their legs might

the crucified broken to quickly bring about their death. Pilate agreed, and the Roman guards broke the legs of the two who were being crucified when Jesus was added. But when they approached Jesus, he was already dead, and therefore there was no need to break his legs. A soldier under Pilate's command used a spear to stab under the fifth rib, and blood and water exited the wound. The beloved disciple who was there saw this and testifies it happened, so you can trust this eyewitness account. The things that happened fulfilled the prophecy that foretold, A bone of him shall not be broken. And again another prophecy said, They shall look on him whom they pierced.

be broken, and that they might be taken away. 32Then came the soldiers, and brake the legs of the first, and of the other which was crucified with him. 33But when they came to Jesus, and saw that he was dead already, they brake not his legs: 34But one of the soldiers with a spear pierced his side, and forthwith came there out blood and water. 35And he that saw it bare record, and his record is true: and he knoweth that he saith true, that ye might believe. 36For these things were done, that the scripture should be fulfilled, A bone of him shall not be broken. 37And again another scripture saith, They shall look on him whom they pierced.

19After his death, Joseph of Arimathea, a secret follower of Jesus who was afraid of the Jews, asked Pilate if he could take the body of Jesus. Pilate permitted him to take Jesus' body. He went, and Nicodemus (who had also visited Jesus in secret) accompanied him and brought a hundred pounds of myrrh mixed with aloes, used by Jews to cover bodies when buried. They covered the body with the mixture and wrapped it with linen to bury him. Near to the place where crucifixions were done, there was a garden. In that garden was a new sepulcher never before used. They laid the body of Jesus there because it was nearby, and the time for the holy feast was approaching.

38And after this Joseph of Arimathæa, being a disciple of Jesus, but secretly for fear of the Jews, besought Pilate that he might take away the body of Jesus: and Pilate gave him leave. He came therefore, and took the body of Jesus. 39And there came also Nicodemus, which at the first came to Jesus by night, and brought a mixture of myrrh and aloes, about an hundred pound weight. 40Then took they the body of Jesus, and wound it in linen clothes with the spices, as the manner of the Jews is to bury. 41Now in the place where he was crucified there was a garden; and in the garden a new sepulchre, wherein was never man yet laid. 42There laid they Jesus therefore because of the Jews' preparation day; for the sepulchre was nigh at hand.

RE Chapter 12

¹The first day of the week Mary the Elect Lady went in the early morning while it was still dark to the burial sepulcher. She saw the stone was rolled away from the sepulcher, and two angels sitting on it. Then she ran to Simon Peter, who was with the other disciple Jesus loved, and said to them, They have removed the Lord out of the sepulcher, and we do not know where he is now established. Peter and the other disciple departed for the sepulcher, running together. The other disciple outran Peter and arrived first at the sepulcher. And he bent down, and looked in, and saw the linen burial cloths. But he did not enter the tomb. Then Simon Peter joined him, and he went into the sepulcher and saw the linen burial cloths, and also the shroud that covered his body. It was not lying with the other burial cloths. Instead it was folded and set down alone. Then the other disciple who arrived first, also entered the sepulcher, and he saw the empty tomb and believed. They still did not understand the prophecy that he must rise again from the dead. Then the disciples departed to return home.

²But Mary stood outside the sepulcher weeping. And as she wept, she bent down and looked into the sepulcher. She saw two angels in white, the one at the head, and the other at the feet where the body of Jesus had lain. They asked her, Woman, why are you mourning? She answered them, Because someone has removed the body of my Lord, and I do not know where

KJV Chapter 20

¹The first day of the week cometh Mary Magdalene early, when it was yet dark, unto the sepulchre, and seeth the stone taken away from the sepulchre. ²Then she runneth, and cometh to Simon Peter, and to the other disciple, whom Jesus loved, and saith unto them, They have taken away the Lord out of the sepulchre, and we know not where they have laid him. ³Peter therefore went forth, and that other disciple, and came to the sepulchre. ⁴So they ran both together: and the other disciple did outrun Peter, and came first to the sepulchre. ⁵And he stooping down, and looking in, saw the linen clothes lying; yet went he not in. ⁶Then cometh Simon Peter following him, and went into the sepulchre, and seeth the linen clothes lie, ⁷And the napkin, that was about his head, not lying with the linen clothes, but wrapped together in a place by itself. ⁸Then went in also that other disciple, which came first to the sepulchre, and he saw, and believed. ⁹For as yet they knew not the scripture, that he must rise again from the dead. ¹⁰Then the disciples went away again unto their own home.

¹¹But Mary stood without at the sepulchre weeping: and as she wept, she stooped down, and looked into the sepulchre, ¹²And seeth two angels in white sitting, the one at the head, and the other at the feet, where the body of Jesus had lain. ¹³And they say unto her, Woman, why weepest thou? She saith unto them, Because they have taken away my Lord, and I know

he is now. After she said this, she walked away and then saw Jesus standing in the garden area. She failed to recognize that it was Jesus. Jesus asked her, Woman, why are you mourning? Who are you looking for? She assumed he was tending the garden, and answered, Sir, if you have taken him away, tell me where he is, and I will claim him. Jesus said to her, Mary.

3She raised her face, recognized him, and addressed him, Greatest of Teachers, which is to say, My Lord. They embraced and Jesus told her, You cannot hold me here. I need to ascend right now to my Father. Go to my followers and say to them, I ascend to my Father and your Father, and to my God and your God.

4Mary the Elect Lady came and told the disciples that she had seen the Lord, and that He had spoken these things to her.

5Later on that same first day of the week, in the evening, when the doors of the room in which the disciples were meeting were closed and locked because of their fear of the Sanhedrin, Jesus came and stood in the middle of this group, and said to them, Peace be with you. And when He said this, He showed to them His hands and His side to prove it was He. Then the disciples were overjoyed, as they beheld their Lord. Jesus repeated to them, Peace be with you. As My Father has sent Me, even so I send you. And after He said this, He breathed upon them, and said to them, I convey to you the Holy

not where they have laid him. 14And when she had thus said, she turned herself back, and saw Jesus standing, and knew not that it was Jesus. 15Jesus saith unto her, Woman, why weepest thou? whom seekest thou? She, supposing him to be the gardener, saith unto him, Sir, if thou have borne him hence, tell me where thou hast laid him, and I will take him away. 16Jesus saith unto her, Mary.

She turned herself, and saith unto him, Rabboni; which is to say, Master. 17Jesus saith unto her, Touch me not; for I am not yet ascended to my Father: but go to my brethren, and say unto them, I ascend unto my Father, and your Father; and to my God, and your God.

18Mary Magdalene came and told the disciples that she had seen the Lord, and that he had spoken these things unto her.

19Then the same day at evening, being the first day of the week, when the doors were shut where the disciples were assembled for fear of the Jews, came Jesus and stood in the midst, and saith unto them, Peace be unto you. 20And when he had so said, he shewed unto them his hands and his side. Then were the disciples glad, when they saw the Lord. 21Then said Jesus to them again, Peace be unto you: as my Father hath sent me, even so send I you. 22And when he had said this, he breathed on them, and saith unto them, Receive ye the Holy Ghost: 23Whose soever sins ye remit, they are remitted

Ghost. Whoever's sins you remit, they are remitted to them; and whoever's sins you retain, they are retained.

unto them; and whose soever sins ye retain, they are retained.

6But Thomas called Didymus, one of the twelve, was absent when Jesus visited them. The other disciples relayed to him, We have seen the Lord. But he responded, Except I also see in his hands the print of the nails, and put my finger into the print of the nails, and thrust my hand into his side, I will not believe. And eight days after this, His disciples were in the same room again, and Thomas with them. Again the doors were locked, and again Jesus came and stood in the middle, and said, Peace be with you. Then He said to Thomas, Reach out your finger and touch my hands. Reach out your hand and feel my injured side. Do not be faithless, but be believing. And Thomas answered and said unto Him, My Lord and my God! Jesus said to him, Thomas, because you have seen me, you believe. Blessed are they that have not seen, and yet believe.

24But Thomas, one of the twelve, called Didymus, was not with them when Jesus came. 25The other disciples therefore said unto him, We have seen the Lord. But he said unto them, Except I shall see in his hands the print of the nails, and put my finger into the print of the nails, and thrust my hand into his side, I will not believe. 26And after eight days again his disciples were within, and Thomas with them: then came Jesus, the doors being shut, and stood in the midst, and said, Peace be unto you. 27Then saith he to Thomas, Reach hither thy finger, and behold my hands; and reach hither thy hand, and thrust it into my side: and be not faithless, but believing. 28And Thomas answered and said unto him, My Lord and my God. 29Jesus saith unto him, Thomas, because thou hast seen me, thou hast believed: blessed are they that have not seen, and yet have believed.

7And there were many other signs that His disciples witnessed that testified of Jesus, but which are not contained in this account. But what is recorded is to testify that Jesus is the Messiah, the Son of God, so that you may obtain Eternal lives, worlds without end through His name.

30And many other signs truly did Jesus in the presence of his disciples, which are not written in this book: 31But these are written, that ye might believe that Jesus is the Christ, the Son of God; and that believing ye might have life through his name.

8I am the one who has testified in this account. And after the many other testimonies of Him, this is my testimony most recent of them all: I saw his glory that He was in the beginning before the world was. Therefore, in the beginning the Word was, for He was the Word, even the messenger of salvation – The light and the Redeemer of the world, the Spirit of truth, who came into the world because the world was made by Him, and in Him was the life of men and the light of men. The worlds were made by Him. Men were made by Him. All things were made by Him, and through Him, and of Him.

9And I, John, bear record that: I beheld His glory, as the glory of the Only Begotten of the Father. He was full of grace and truth, even the Spirit of truth. He came and dwelt in the flesh, and lived among us.

10And I, John, saw that He received not of the fullness at the first, but received grace for grace. And He received not of the fullness at first, but continued from grace to grace, until He received a fullness. And in this way He qualified to be called to become the Son of God, because He received not of the fullness at the first.

11And I, John, bear record, and lo the Heavens were opened, and the Holy Ghost descended upon Him in the form of a dove and remained upon Him. There came a voice out of Heaven saying: You are my Beloved Son, this day I have begotten you; for I was there with John

KJV Chapter 21

24This is the disciple which testifieth of these things, and wrote these things: and we know that his testimony is true.

the Baptist when he baptized Jesus.

¹²And I, John, bear record that He received a fullness of the glory of the Father. And He received all power, both in Heaven and on earth, and the glory of the Father was with Him, for he dwelt in Him.

¹³The Father testified of Jesus also on the Mount, when He was transfigured before us, and the glory of Heaven was upon Him, and we saw Him enter the Heavenly realm. The Father testified also when our Lord prayed for those who do follow Him. And the Holy Ghost has and does testify of Him to all who receive Him. Therefore, we know by irrefutable evidence that Jesus is the Messiah, sent to fulfill prophecy, and to lead all who will follow through the path of His Father.

¹⁴After this Jesus showed Himself again to the disciples at the Sea of Tiberias. This is an account of that event: There were together Simon Peter, and Thomas called Didymus, and Nathanael from the city of Cana in Galilee, and the sons of Zebedee, and two others, also disciples. Simon Peter said to them, I ascend to the deep. They responded to him, We go with you. They went forth, and entered into the ark; and they could not grasp anything.

¹After these things Jesus shewed himself again to the disciples at the sea of Tiberias; and on this wise shewed he himself. ²There were together Simon Peter, and Thomas called Didymus, and Nathanael of Cana in Galilee, and the sons of Zebedee, and two other of his disciples. ³Simon Peter saith unto them, I go a fishing. They say unto him, We also go with thee. They went forth, and entered into a ship immediately; and that night they caught nothing.

15But at the horizon of the morning star, Jesus stood at the sacred entry; however the disciples could not recognize it was Jesus for the glory about Him. Then Jesus asked them, Children, have you celebrated the ritual meal? They answered Him, No. And He directed them and said, Approach the veil to the east and you will find what you seek. They approached the veil as instructed, and now they were overcome by the multitude of what was received. Therefore the disciple Jesus loved said to Peter, It is the Lord. Now when Simon Peter heard that it was the Lord, he quickly clothed himself (for he did not wear the apparel), and cast himself into the great deep. And the other disciples came into the ark and parted also the veil (for they were not bound by the limits of this world).

16As they ascended, they saw a fire burning at the offering place and the Flesh Offering was upon it, who is also the Bread of Life. Jesus said to them, Rise above the flesh you now occupy, and Simon Peter ascended, and drew the veil open, and there were ministering a hundred, and then fifty, and then three; and for these many who they beheld, yet the veil remained open.

17Jesus said to them, Come and eat the food of the rising sun. And none of the disciples asked of him, What name is now yours? knowing that it was their Lord. Jesus then served to them His flesh and blood, and they were filled by His Spirit. This was now the third time Jesus

4But when the morning was now come, Jesus stood on the shore: but the disciples knew not that it was Jesus. 5Then Jesus saith unto them, Children, have ye any meat? They answered him, No. 6And he said unto them, Cast the net on the right side of the ship, and ye shall find. They cast therefore, and now they were not able to draw it for the multitude of fishes. 7Therefore that disciple whom Jesus loved saith unto Peter, It is the Lord. Now when Simon Peter heard that it was the Lord, he girt his fisher's coat unto him, (for he was naked,) and did cast himself into the sea. 8And the other disciples came in a little ship; (for they were not far from land, but as it were two hundred cubits,) dragging the net with fishes.

9As soon then as they were come to land, they saw a fire of coals there, and fish laid thereon, and bread. 10Jesus saith unto them, Bring of the fish which ye have now caught. 11Simon Peter went up, and drew the net to land full of great fishes, an hundred and fifty and three: and for all there were so many, yet was not the net broken.

12Jesus saith unto them, Come and dine. And none of the disciples durst ask him, Who art thou? knowing that it was the Lord. 13Jesus then cometh, and taketh bread, and giveth them, and fish likewise. 14This is now the third time that Jesus shewed himself to his disci-

ministered to His disciples following His rise from among the dead.

[18]After the meal, Jesus said to Simon Peter, Simon, son of Jonas, do you love me above every thing else? He answered him, Yes, Lord. You know that I love you. He said to him, Take care of my lambs as they are growing. He asked him again the second time, Simon, son of Jonas, do you love me above every thing else? He said to Him, Yes, Lord you know that I love you. He said to him, Take care of my lambs as they increase. He said to him the third time, Simon, son of Jonas, do you love me above every thing else? Peter was concerned because He asked him for a third time, Do you love me? And he said to Him, Lord, you know all things. You know that I love you. Jesus said to him, Care for my lambs as they are added upon. In the name of Father Ahman I tell you, when you were progressing, you dressed yourself, and went where you chose to go; but as you approach the end of the path, you will have to let others stretch out your hands and likewise nail you, even if you plead to have the bitter cup removed. This He said to foretell the sacrificial death that is required for endless glory. And then He added, You must follow after me.

[19]Then Peter turned and looked at the disciple whom Jesus loved, who was behind. This was him who was next to Jesus at supper, and had quietly asked Him during supper, Lord, who is the one that will betray you? Peter saw him and asked Jesus, Lord, and what will become of this man? Jesus ex-

ples, after that he was risen from the dead.

[15]So when they had dined, Jesus saith to Simon Peter, Simon, son of Jonas, lovest thou me more than these? He saith unto him, Yea, Lord; thou knowest that I love thee. He saith unto him, Feed my lambs. [16]He saith to him again the second time, Simon, son of Jonas, lovest thou me? He saith unto him, Yea, Lord; thou knowest that I love thee. He saith unto him, Feed my sheep. [17]He saith unto him the third time, Simon, son of Jonas, lovest thou me? Peter was grieved because he said unto him the third time, Lovest thou me? And he said unto him, Lord, thou knowest all things; thou knowest that I love thee. Jesus saith unto him, Feed my sheep.

[18]Verily, verily, I say unto thee, When thou wast young, thou girdedst thyself, and walkedst whither thou wouldest: but when thou shalt be old, thou shalt stretch forth thy hands, and another shall gird thee, and carry thee whither thou wouldest not. [19]This spake he, signifying by what death he should glorify God. And when he had spoken this, he saith unto him, Follow me.

[20]Then Peter, turning about, seeth the disciple whom Jesus loved following; which also leaned on his breast at supper, and said, Lord, which is he that betrayeth thee?

[21]Peter seeing him saith to Jesus, Lord, and what shall this man do?

plained, I said to him, John, my beloved what do you desire? And John replied, Lord, give to me the power that I may bring souls to you. And I said to him, In the name of Father Ahman I commit to you that because you desire this you shall tarry until I return in my glory.

20And for this reason the Lord said to Peter, if I will that he tarry till I come, what is that to you? For he desires from me that he might bring souls to me, but you desire that you might come to me in my kingdom. I tell you, Peter, yours was a good desire, but my beloved has undertaken a greater work on earth. In the name of Father Ahman I say to you that you shall both have what you requested, and you both will have joy from what you each requested.

21Now, therefore, know that Jesus is the Messiah, the Walker in the Path who has proven for evermore that Father Ahman sent Him into the world to prove His Father's path.

22In addition to this account, many other things were done by Jesus, which, if they were all written, that library would fill the entire cosmos. Amen.

22Jesus saith unto him, If I will that he tarry till I come, what is that to thee? follow thou me. 23Then went this saying abroad among the brethren, that that disciple should not die: yet Jesus said not unto him, He shall not die; but, If I will that he tarry till I come, what is that to thee?

25And there are also many other things which Jesus did, the which, if they should be written every one, I suppose that even the world itself could not contain the books that should be written. Amen.